How to ge
SPONSORSHIP
for motorsport

June Laird

A FOULIS Motoring Book
First published 1986

Published by:
Haynes Publishing Group
Sparkford, Near Yeovil, Somerset BA22
7JJ

British Library Cataloguing in Publication Data
Laird, June
  How to get sponsorship for motorsport.
  1. Motorsports—Sponsorship—Great
  Britain
  I. Title
  796.7'079   GV1019.5.G7

    ISBN 0-85429-536-4

Editor: Robert Iles
Page layout: Mike King
Printed in England by: J.H.Haynes & Co. Ltd.

Contents

Foreword by Derek Bell		5
Acknowledgements		6
Illustrations		7
Introduction		9
Appendices		11
Chapter one	Sponsorship: The 'Name' on the Game	12
Chapter two	The Necessity for Support	16
Chapter three	Sponsorship: Types of and Eligibility for	20
Chapter four	The Preliminary Research	26
Chapter five	Preparing your Approach	35
Chapter six	Approaching a Prospective Sponsor and Negotiating a Sponsorship	57
Chapter seven	The Publicity Return and Contract	72
Chapter eight	Advertising and Sponsorship Agencies	85
Chapter nine	Rules of the 'Game'	90
Chapter ten	Sponsorship Through the Eyes of its Participants	96
Author's Summary		100

McLaren's latest formula one car – along with its drivers Alain Prost and Keke Rosberg – combine to show clearly their sponsors' names on both man and machine.

Foreword by Derek Bell

Twice winner of the World Endurance Championship and four times Le Mans winner

Sponsorship, it seems to me, has been a fact of life throughout my career. How well I remember the Gold Leaf Team Lotus in 1968. At this time I was attempting the move from Formula 3 to Formula 2 and assuming I would get a drive on my ability alone, but as a young up and coming driver I had no idea as to the implications of acquiring sponsors.

I had written to numerous companies convinced that they would jump at the opportunity to invest money in this unknown driver. How wrong I was, the only encouragement I got was a badge from a reputable car hire company with the words, 'We Try Harder' printed on it!

Since those days I have been only too aware of the problems facing young drivers trying to raise money to follow their passion for motorsport. I frequently receive 'phone calls from people asking for my advice, and it is not easy to help.

I have always found it unpleasant to try to sell myself to a faceless character in the marketing department of a large company, who hasn't the first idea or interest in motorsport; to me it's a distinctly demoralizing situation.

Raising sponsorship will always be difficult, but I feel the information this book offers can only help bewildered sponsor seekers.

One last word though; having found your sponsor, do look after him, so many people don't, much to the detriment of our sport.

Acknowledgements

This book could not have been written without reference to others both in terms of inspiration and direct help. In this respect I should, first, like to thank those companies who have, down the seasons, contributed towards my own track record.

Avon Tyres, the Bristol Street Group, Britax Excelsior, Tony Brooks Motors of Weybridge, Broughton Motors Northants, Bury & Hopwood of Stockport, Castrol Sport, the Chase Hotel Nuneaton, Erskine Fire Equipment, R. Gander Transport of Henfield, Griffin Helmets, Henfield Motors, John Hosmer Motors of Hemel Hempstead, JCT 600 of Bradford, Jaybrand Accessories, Knibbs of Manchester, Koni Dampers, Lancia UK, Lookers Grosvenor of Preston, Lucas Batteries, Lucas-Girling, Vin Malkie of Manchester, Martini & Rossi, NGK, H.R. Owen of London, Prontaprint of Blackpool/Leeds/Lytham/Northampton/Sale, Ritchies of Glasgow, Rosche Racewear, S & G Motors of Arundel, Savoir Fare of Hinckley, Shell UK Oils, Shell Petroleum, Mike Spence Motors of Reading, H.M. Stevenson of Ayr, H.M. Stevenson of Tullibody, the Tilley Group of Brighton, Travelfar Coach Tours of Henfield, G.E. Tunbridge of Tunbridge Wells and Warner Motors of Gloucester.

Secondly, I should like to thank all those who have contributed to the publication of this book:

ABC Advertising, Atlantic Computers PLC, the BARC, Castrol Sport, Delta Racing, Endeavour of Brighton, the Financial Times, John Foulston, Harringtons of Brighton, Lotus Cars, Antonia Loysen BWRDC, Lucas Batteries, Lucas-Girling, McLaren International Racing, Martini & Rossi, Steve Rubell Publicity, Shell UK Oils, the Knibbs Group, and the Tordoff Motor Group.

The author wishes to convey her special thanks to those firms and photographers who have very kindly donated their work to this book:
Andrew Ferguson of 'Club Team Lotus.'
Frank E. Hall.
McLaren International in conjunction with Marlboro' Tobacco. Fred Scatley in association with John Foulston, Atlantic Computers PLC and the Haslemere Sports and Racing Car Centre.

I should finally like to convey my thanks to Frank Hall of Sale for his fine photographic contribution and to Bill Wood of Leicestercard-Mallock fame. Bill may not realize it, but his comments regarding my heavily bedecalled Lancia, and whether it really did represent sponsors or whether the decals were there merely to hold the car in one piece, can truthfully be said to be the words that set my thoughts a-buzzing ... Prescott 1983.

Illustrations

Frontispiece   Marlboro' McLaren

Chapter one   The Riley Furnishings/Harper Brothers Mallock U2

Chapter one   Bill Wood's Leicestercard Mallock.

Chapter two   Ian Hughes of BMW fame once rallied this well signed Escort Mark 2.

Chapter two   Longstanding combination, the John Players Special Lotus formula one.

Chapter three   The author's well supported Lancia Fulvia Lusso 1.6

Chapter three   Trade support clearly depicted on John Istead's Mallock U2.

Chapter four   Mike Kerr's 'Stage' Chevette showing space for sale on the bonnet.

Chapter four   Another view of the author's Lancia; this time the 'poor' end!

Chapter five   Antonia Loysen at the wheel.

Chapter five   Antonia Loysen in action.

Chapter six   Barry William's Ford Fiesta, a graphic artist's dream.

Chapter six   Multi-Sponsorship, the Lancia-Martini record breaking Delta Turbo 1.6HF.

Chapter seven   A double for Guyson Euroblast who support both Harewood speed hillclimb and Jim Thomson's Pilbeam.

Chapter seven   Circuit sponsorship: Oulton Park.

Chapter eight   Tricky logo, John Meredith's Clan Crusader.

Chapter eight   Main sponsorship requires clarity; a clear example being Vince O'Mahoney's BMW.

Chapter nine   Giving a sponsor value for money, the Peter Clement's Shell Oils/Super Cleaners Talbot.

Chapter ten   The real McCoy, Porsche at Le Mans.

Chapter ten   John Foulston's McLaren still wears the logo of its one time successful sponsor 'Yardley for Men.'

Introduction

It has been said that there are three reasons for writing a book; the dole queue. unquenchable inspiration or irresistible temptation. In my case all three have had some bearing: I have time on my hands, a state resulting from my occupation, rather than from the lack of one; I am a participant in motorsport with, I am informed, a reputation for hunting and bagging sponsors; and I also suffer both anger, and elation: anger at those competitors and organisers who mistakenly believe that to a woman the word 'Sponsor' is synonymous with 'Sugar Daddy', and elation on those occasions when I do bag a sponsor.

Though I have had a reasonable amount of success in the quest for my own sponsorship, I do not feel that my 'secret' formula should be jealously guarded. Fundamental to success, is to ensure that every approach follows a carefully deliberated plan or 'modus operandi.' Though, perhaps justifiably, considered by many participants as somewhat soul destroying, following just such a plan is the premier way of reducing the high average of approach refusals.

When starting the hunt for sponsors it should be understood that in this imperfect world of humans, to quote that Yorkshire adage, 'Yer don't get owt for nowt, unless yer do it for yer sen!' You can't expect the local butcher to agree to putting up the price of his offal to fund sponsorship for your racing just because you yourself happen to believe that you are 'God's gift' to Formula Ford 1600, and because you have managed to finish one race unscathed. Nor can you expect the local tycoon to be the least bit impressed by your Saville Row suit, instant printshop prospectus and your 'big talk', if it can be deduced easily that your claims have little or no foundation. The butcher might happily increase his prices if he can be convinced that the return you are offering might induce non-customers to change to his brand of 'slaughter house produce'. Likewise, the tycoon may help if, in turn, you can convince him that his half million really will produce another half, or more, and that you really are the reincarnation of Rudolf Caracciola. Readiness for sponsorship hunting rests entirely with the candidate, be he an individual or the representative of a club. No one is waiting for you to call; on the contrary, sponsorship is more often than not a case of 'don't call us, we'll call you!'

Likewise, don't be seen as being a Promenade Percy; zooming up to Burlington Berty's emporium at a 100 knots in your Porsche 911 will certainly not convince your prospect that you're another Derek Bell. It is more likely that you'll be thanked for your interest, wished good luck and dismissed with the silent thought that you can go and break your neck at someone else's expense!

Sponsorship is not on offer by demand, nor is it the right of every sportsman and woman. Moreover it is not something to be

9

treated lightly when successfully established. It is very much a matter of give and take, with probably much more giving than taking. It is not the recipe for instant stardom, but solely a means of bettering your own efforts secondary to promoting the business of your sponsor.

I hope within the Chapters of this book to be able to pass on some of the tips and, for want of a better term, 'tricks of the trade' which will enable you to find the support as I am reputed to have done. Listed separately are all those who have made my 'game' that much more pleasant and easy, and who have, each and every one, inspired the writing of this book. I have also written in the hope that it might also interest firms eager to know more about this aspect of motorsport. Similarly, the contents may also be of help to many sporting participants other than those of its motoring direction.

Good luck to all who seek their own particular answer within the pages which follow; may your car or club caravan soon be held together, like mine, with decals.

June Laird, author 1985

Appendices

Chapter five

Specimen sponsorship prospectus, Miss Antonia Loysen.
Specimen letter of introduction to a main sponsor.

Appendix A: Letter to a nominal sponsor with publicity return.
Appendix B: Letter to product sponsor for advertising rights with publicity return.
Appendix C: Letter to product sponsor for accessories and nominal cash support with publicity return.
Appendix C2:   Letter from a product sponsor replying to a request for advertising/accessory backing.

Chapter six

Appendix D: Why motorsport?
Appendix E: Specimen sponsorship invoice and remittance advice.
Appendix F: Specimen sponsorship contract.
Appendix G: Example of how a trade sponsor's name might be used.
Appendix H: Reply to a request for sponsorship.

Chapter seven

Appendix J: Sponsorship agreement in letter form.
Appendix K: Specimen product sponsor's advertisement embodying the success of their sponsorship liaison.
Appendix L: Letter to a participant showing a sponsor's appreciation of the former's efforts on their behalf.
Appendix M: Specimen press release.

Chapter ten

Appendix N: Some successful sponsorships, past and present.

Chapter 1

Sponsorship: The 'Name' on the Game

In choosing a title for this opening Chapter, it is the word 'NAME' which might be seen as being the operative one, and one that, in a definitive sense, subtly hides the whole purpose of sponsorship. Therefore, when looking at the range of present day sport it is 'names' like Cornhill Test and JPS Lotus which have become the norm. The former indicating Cornhill Insurance's support of test cricket, whilst John Players Special cigarettes currently sponsor the Lotus formula one team.

Before considering the subject of sponsorship it is essential for us all to recognise that the days have gone when to take part in sport, either as a serious amateur or full-time professional, one needed to be well-heeled or selected to become what was then referred to as a 'works' driver, reliant upon fees, a share of the prize money and such personal advertising as was allowed. In the 1980s it is doubtful if many of our up-and-coming young sportsmen even know that there was such a period in our sporting history and, of course, all are much too young to have experienced it. This, however, is not the case with myself. My first experience of the 'name' being linked to anything remotely connected with entertainment came towards the end of world war two. Playing host to our American allies one became used to the strains of radio programmes produced expressly for GIs by the American Forces Network; AFN for short. One of the programme's presenters would open a show with the introduction that, for example, 'the Coca Cola Company Presents.' Similarly, another American institution, the Glenn Miller Orchestra of the early forties, simply relied upon Chesterfield cigarettes since it was a fact that to provide the best in entertainment a radio station needed money. This was obtained by selling air advertising space in such a way that the show would be instantly connected with the advertiser.

The foregoing, of course, only applied to our friends from over the 'pond'. In Britain anything of this nature being considered both cheap and unnecessary. The amateur did not advertise at all and radio was seen as being purely an entertainment/news medium, whose acts were very often seen as being corny and sometimes even second rate. On the sports field our competitors were more often than not beaten by better trained and better prepared adversaries: such being true of our athletes, boxers, tennis players and, yes, even our racing drivers. Racing car manufacturers lacked money and many went to the wall with only the best-heeled remaining to begin the long term process of flying the flag. Names like Cooper, Jaguar, Lotus and MG kept going, whilst firms like Alta, Connaught and ERA disappeared, although, eventually the latter company was to become the basis for the BRM organisation. Cricketers, footballers and golfers, even of professional status, had to rely on out-of-season coaching in order to make ends meet. This lack of finance affected training facilities and playing facilities, and as a result the quality of performance. Once again our American cousins dominated athletics, boxing and tennis, the Aussies dominated cricket and the Latins dominated motor racing due, often, to government support, financial support and an atmosphere within their own Country which created the will to win.

Since this book deals with motorsport, it is with this in mind that we must now investigate the changes which have made this publication a necessity. The fifties saw the first of many changes; travel becoming more widespread with the development of the world's airline network, and foreign car manufacturers recognising talent amongst many of our own drivers; the likes of Peter Collins, Mike Hawthorn and Stirling Moss soon being seen at the wheels of the works Ferraris, Maseratis and Mercedes-Benz. However, the biggest event of the decade and the one destined to have the most profound effect on our way of life was the introduction of domestic TV. Yet another change in our British way of life is that which confronted our industrial bosses. The advent of peace and the need to preserve it generated an increase in trade between countries worldwide. It soon became obvious that if the British were to

The name well and truly 'On' the game. Speed events stars Peter and Ray Harper share the 'Riley's Furnishings' Mallock U2.

be anything of a success in this new world, in partnership with Europe, we would need to rethink the entire technique of marketing on the Continent: and so the concluding years of the decade were to see the introduction of British commercial television.

Supporters of the sober British status quo, and more especially those who had experience of the American variety, held up their hands in horror. There were visions of programmes being introduced with ... 'Corona presents,' or being relentlessly interrupted with instructions to 'Smoke Players' and 'Drink Oxo!' We need not have worried, for in keeping with our best

The motoring press refer to Scottish hillclimb ace Bill Wood's car as the 'Leicestercard Mallock', an example of name linking.

traditions we were carefully, and tactfully, led into the ways of the new medium. Some years later came the introduction of commercial radio destined to have a similar impact at more local level.

Eventually with the 1960s well under way, it became 'academic' that the next move would be a fresh look at sport. If broadcasting and television could benefit from the inevitable cash injection, so too could our sports personalities, organisers and facilities. However, the first really successful motoring venture to benefit from sponsorship advertising is recognised as being Yardley BRM and later Yardley McLaren. Anxious to diversify into male cosmetics, Yardley saw the male dominated Grand Prix formula as being an ideal way to launch their new product. By the late '60s this advertising bug had spread to all forms of motorsport, whilst eventually

embracing many almost unfollowed pastimes such as basketball, darts and even snooker. In our sport we were to see the traditional British Racing Green being replaced with 'Jacob's Coat of Many Colours;' sponsorship European style had arrived.

What then is sponsorship? It is principally an injection of cash in return for the beneficiary exposing the donor to the public at large by simply displaying and linking their name and product alongside, or in conjunction with, that of themselves. It is an investment which can benefit the competitor's ability and capability, the sponsorship when used efficiently virtually guaranteeing, at least, a modicum of success. The exposure can, likewise, benefit both parties through the resultant press, radio and television reference, as well as that within the public eye. The effectiveness to both sides being dependent upon the cash invested, which is in turn dependent upon the status of the event, the participant and the sponsor. That sponsorship is an American institution cannot be denied, but that it has done much good cannot be overlooked either. Our competitiveness, standards and facilities in every sport have improved to an extent far beyond the dreams of our forebears. Unhappily for sport there will always be an element of greed and dubious behaviour. This only applies however to a small minority and happily for motorsport the misdemeanours are minimal.

There can be no greater tribute to the usefulness of the sponsorship system than our success in many international and worldwide competitions in recent years: the list is endless and encompasses just about every conceivable sporting activity. In motor racing itself Britain and the Commonwealth have entered the names of no fewer than eight world champions into the record book, some more than once. In this respect it should be noted that the first, Mike Hawthorn, achieved this accolade without sponsorship and although he was admittedly a works driver, this was an entirely different matter in 1958. It might well be argued that but for the advent of sponsorship we might still be awaiting the discovery of both a competitive car and, in addition, world champion number two.

Likewise, we have produced many top-class drivers in all forms of motorsport; names like Derek Bell, Johnny Dumfries, Richard Noble, Alastair Douglas-Osborne, Tony Pond and Nigel Mansell are but a few who have achieved success in the worlds of endurance racing, Formula 3, land-speed records, speed-eventing, rallying and, top of them all, Formula 1. Similarly, our lady racing drivers too have made an impact on the sport, sponsorship having helped the likes of Louise Aitken-Walker in the field of rallying, Davina Gallica in the double roll of racing driver/skier and Gillian Fortescue-Thomas in speed-events. From a personal standpoint, I was honoured with the captaincy in 1985 of the Lancia-Martini Record Project in which my team of four lady drivers, Linda Elmes, Dee Knight, Antonia Loysen and myself, successfully re-established ten outright United Kingdom National records for cars in Class 'E' (1501cc to 2000cc). Our success was made possible because of the considerable support given to us by a total of over twenty sponsors.

Sponsorship is not a gift, nor is it a form of begging. It is a necessity if our sportsmen and sportswomen are to remain at the top.

Chapter 2

The Necessity for Support

Post-war motoring competitor and author C.A.N. May, once told me that writing a book is dependent on two things: first, the completion of Chapter one and second, the utilisation of that Chapter as the basis from which the subsequent text will follow. Having described the birth of sponsorship in the United Kingdom, together with a brief analysis of what it is, the next step is for us to examine the necessity for it.

Reverting once again to history, especially that of Great Britain, we will all appreciate that being, as we once were, a part of the world's greatest Empire, presented us with the unique opportunity to trade within that Union in an almost unchallenged way. Markets were virtually established and administered at will and we didn't have to look far in order to create our export trade. In the main we bought and sold within the Empire, in which one member nation was almost reliant upon another. Due to this somewhat complacent state of affairs advertising and publicity were therefore low-key factors of our everyday life and were only used as a method of exposing firms and their products, and for convincing the consumer that one brand might be better than another.

Having tried very briefly to show, as far as the UK is concerned, that our trade at international level was almost totally se-cure and unhindered, now we must examine those changes that would have a bearing upon our future commercial lives and sporting pastimes. In concluding this brief look at the past, advertising and publicity at all levels of sophistication had to survive and to thrive upon large roadside hoardings, neon displays, personal recommendation, the media and the never to be forgotten sandwich board.

In order that I can come to the point of this Chapter more expeditiously, I will ask you to accept that the two most significant changes in European trading techniques were, first, the many status alterations affecting countries worldwide: for example India on the one hand and Japan on the other. Second, the need to preserve peace at any price and not least by massive economic means.

Naturally this 'gi-normous' increase in international trading has manifested its own problems; how do you sell into a market that offers so many alternatives? How do you become a brand leader? How, more simply, do you remain in business surrounded by such competition? Quality and service only solve a small part of the question and, good as both may be, they do not add up to volume sales. The only way to achieve this aim was for every commercial undertaking to adopt the American style of trading now termed

Longstanding combination: Ayrton Senna's John Player Special Lotus photographed during the 1985 Brazilian Grand Prix.

'marketing;' the techniques which apply being adaptable product to product and nation to nation, but basically embodying the qualities of sound advertising, promotion, public relations, publicity, research and good old-fashioned salesmanship. With its acceptance in Europe has come all the trappings of colour advertising, commercial colour television, commercial radio, market research, public acceptance and, finally, sponsorship. In fact it can be said that many firms actually resort to a form of 'brainwashing' in order to get their message across and not least do they see the teenager as being among the most susceptible of all the targets of their campaigns. As to how one remains in business, this is a different story: in short, our own country has had to follow the American way of business in which only the fittest survive.

Keeping up with the marketing impact has become the domaine of the advertising and public relations experts whose terms of reference in Europe and the United Kingdom are akin to those of their American counterparts. On the subject of advertising, this itself has become much more liberal allowing the exploitation of both the female and male form to emphasise clothing, cosmetics, furniture and even travel whilst, similarly, on any shopping day you may find yourself accosted by teams of market research interviewers acting for, and on behalf of, the PR consultants. Looking further afield for even fresher avenues, it had been known for some time that British sport was very much in the doldrums with the worst affected being cricket and boxing. Both needed, not only cash, but an inducement to restore public interest. In our own field motorsport suffered increasing costs, together with a

17

diminishing number of interested manufacturers. In all sports the participants put the problem down to four things: first, a lack of cash, second, a lack of incentive, third, a lack of both governmental and national interest due to poor results and, fourth, a lack of up-to-date training facilities. The publicity experts were quick to catch on to this need and were soon exploring this avenue of marketing. They found that the apparel, the equipment and, in many cases, the facilities all lent themselves to the task of exposing firms and their products. Welcomed by the competitor and organiser alike, the injection of cash by way of sponsorship, in return for advertising and publicity rights, soon enabled our sportsmen and women to show an improvement far beyond anyone's wildest dreams. Additionally the government also began to take an interest by appointing a

Ian Hughes of BMW fame once rallied this well signed Escort Mk 2.

Cabinet Minister with direct responsibility for sport: this entire catalyst paying off quickly by producing participants in all forms of sporting activity that were to prove the equal of any competition in the world. Referring to our sport, sponsorship saved many small specialist manufacturers, developed new ones and encouraged the formation of professionally administered race and rally schools offering training to both a wider and re-vitalised public. Fees and prize money increased substantially in every sport, with the entire spectrum taking on a distinct professional image even at junior levels. From the sponsors' point of view, companies are able to reap huge benefits and profits from the ever increasing international exposure this medium can bring. In this respect, for example, that predominantly European of motorsporting activities Formula 1 has been able to spread its interest as far afield as Africa, the Americas and the Far East, with the international rallying world following suit.

Our cars can be seen all over the world displaying the logos of such well known firms as Lombard Banking, John Players and Yardley, until now, little known beyond our own shores.

In motorsport sponsors' names and liveries appear on crash hats, overalls, racing and rally cars, in press releases and programmes, at the circuits, rally stages, speed and trials venues: the image of "that's our car" or "that's our driver" now being well established. Cars themselves are displayed in the foyers of airports, hotels and the more prestigious office blocks, whilst a day at the races, for a sponsor and his clientele, no longer means Ascot or Epsom, but also Brands Hatch or Silverstone. In return for backing, a professional racing driver can be found spending his, or her, leisure time promoting and publicising their sponsors business or service; the amateur also benefiting from this form of support and, likewise, taking on a more professional image. Entertaining and the hospitality suite have become the hallmark of the wealthier competitors and 'bigtime' financiers, the tools of their trade acquiring such names as: Guyson-Pilbeam, JPS-Lotus, Lancia-Martini and Rothman's-Porsche. Linking the name is yet another aspect of sponsorship, ensuring a press mention for the sponsor and their business with, in many cases, the link being registered to obviate mis-quotes or deliberate press exclusion. This latter aspect is something I will endeavour to describe later on. However, whilst sport needs these cash incentives it may be argued that, whilst sponsorship does create success, it can sometimes be seen as ruling and dictating the course of its beneficiaries at all levels. Likewise, it is sometimes seen as destroying the very basis of sportsmanship in its truest sense, if allowed to do so.

Having read this Chapter you will all appreciate that the need for sponsorship, has to be the cost to compete. Gone is the day when the club rally driver might count that cost in a few pounds. Gone is the day when all clubs had to fund events from their own koffers. Gone is the day when promotors could rely almost solely on gate-money, trade adverts, works cars and works drivers. The big problem however, facing the motorsport participant is the one of simply finding the sponsor, a 'hazard' in keeping with most things we British undertake. New fashions are slow to catch on in this country, not least amongst them sponsorship; many firms do not understand its function and, worse still, many don't want to. Take some consolation from the fact that there are those who do appreciate the advantages and the potential to be obtained from their participation in a sponsorship programme. No doubt time will serve to mellow the apathy many of us so often find elsewhere.

Chapter 3

Sponsorship: Types of and Eligibility for

Following upon the two previous Chapters, the next step is for me to spend the pages of this Chapter detailing the various types of backing which are available to all motorsport participants. Similarly, I will also describe the requirements that are necessary in order that the same participants or organisers may become suitable sponsor subjects.

Beginning with the types of sponsorship which are available, there are predominantly four: direct support, product support, sponsorship by result and a form of assurance sometimes defined as underwriting. Each of the four variants has an entirely different modus operandi from that of the other three and are described in turn as follows.

First and foremost is the simplest of all four, 'direct sponsorship' or 'support'. This is the variant most favoured by both the individual competitor and the team. In this respect the sum agreed is paid to the subject on the basis of, either, a one-off lump sum or so much 'up-front' and the balance by pre-arranged instalments. Included as part and parcel of the 'direct' style is that which is referred to as advertising or publicity support: this takes the form of an agreed sponsorship fee in respect of space purchased at, or on, anything connected with motorsport.

Second, and also of prime importance to the actual competitor or team, is that which I defined as 'product support.' Not so simple in its application this support usually compliments the 'direct' style. Self-explanatory, the title refers to those companies willing to supply accessories, fuel, oil and spares in return for their name and product being displayed on the competing car or service vehicle, whilst sometimes, in addition, the supporter might also donate a nominal sum of money. However, as with all things that appertain to sponsorship, don't get carried away with the idea that 'product support' is readily available the instant you start competing; in this respect it is certain that your approach to any such company will need to be accompanied by a few substantive results, together with a couple of recent press mentions. Whilst, as I have said, almost totally applicable to either the competitor or team, it can in some cases be applied to a club or organiser as a straight nominal fee in return for venue and other advertising.

Third, and possibly the least popular, 'sponsorship based upon result' is applicable entirely to competitors or teams. This means of gaining financial support is the one favoured by, for example, General Motors Dealersport. Simplified, the participants receive an agreed sum in relation to their individual event placings and/or seasonal championship results. Often disfavoured, its application can create problems and has been known to place considerable strain on the recipient, encouraging, sometimes, a win-at-all-costs attitude.

Finally, and probably the most involved variant, is 'underwritten' sponsorship. Whilst appreciating its application, I am not at all sure why it is that this style of support appeals mainly to clubs; although it is clear why it certainly does not have the blessing of the individual or team. I am therefore left wondering if it has anything to do with club accountancy, whilst appreciating fully the damage that can result when a club becomes involved with an individual competitor and attempts to utilise this type of sponsorship; a fact which I can confirm through a somewhat recent and bitter experience. It does, however, appear to work for the club on its own as well as for larger organisations.

Therefore, what is 'underwritten' sponsorship? I am sure that you all know something of how both bookmakers and insurers transact their respective businesses. In the case of the bookmakers they refer to their method of countering a possible big winner as 'laying-off,' whilst the insurer counters a big risk by 'underwriting' the amount involved and so it is with the club. Having compiled a budget, the club will approach a firm, or number of firms, seeking a guarantee of their backing for the maximum support required. Sometimes the subject will draw the sum agreed in advance: returning any residue, whilst at other times they will await the conclusion of the particular event and will then submit the relevant accounts up to the amount underwritten. In other words the club or organiser 'lays-off', through this style of sponsorship, the risk of any deficit that might arise from one of their promoted events. However, as I have already said, this style of support cannot work where it involves a joint club and individual arrangement, and more especially when the latter finds themself facing an un-expected and extraneous expense not foreseen during negotiations. Of course it might well be that the particular club or organisation has to make a tax return, in which case prudence will dictate the amount of income disclosed. This could well be the reason why it is favoured only by clubs and organisers, and why it is totally unacceptable to the individual competitor or team.

The second part of this Chapter deals with the eligibility and qualification of the sponsor applicants be they a club, a competitor, an organiser or a team. In this respect it is only right that there has to be some standard since sponsorship is not an entitlement, but primarily a privilege. It is no good anyone thinking that around every corner lurks a benefactor just waiting to hand out money to every Tom, Dick, Harry or Mary on the basis that he, or she, simply wants to drive a race or rally car; however good you may think you are. Such a requirement is, of course, a factor which governs many aspects of life itself and although quite categorical in its general sponsorship application, there are exceptions to the rule as it applies to any club or organising body. I feel, therefore, that it will benefit the context of this section if I deal, first, with the eligibility requirements of the latter two mentioned.

Since the majority of car clubs and organisers have been in existence for many years, this factor alone has afforded both these subjects the opportunity to build up their identity and their respective track records. Consequently it should be a comparatively easy matter for them to attract sponsorship without too much hassle, since both should have an impressive and established curriculum vitae. Additionally, they should likewise be known for either their local affiliations or from their national status, for example: The *British* Racing Drivers Club, The *Lancashire and Cheshire* Car Club or The *Daily* Express; the latter from the organisational side of things. Similarly, most motoring associations solely seek support for a specific event or series, thus making their needs that much more readily obtainable than those of the average competitor. Unfortunately this state of affairs is often seen as being a 'bone of contention' between the subjects under discussion and the latter mentioned, and more so when the club or organiser accepts, or seeks, a small sum from a large source. This can give the false impression that motorsport can be bought into cheaply, whilst also spoiling the future chances the competitor or team might have of approaching the same company, or companies. Likewise, an organiser is able to use their influence to attract sponsors from amongst their own colleagues, customers and suppliers.

For the purpose of substantiating my claim that clubs and the like should not find sponsor-hunting too much of a problem, I would like to take this opportunity of relating to you an experience with which I was personally involved. A few years ago I was approached by the Chairman of a reasonably well known club with something of a desperate plea. The club's biggest annual event was only five weeks away and they had just been informed that their expected continuing support had been rescinded due to a change in the sponsor's policy. With many items due for clarification and printing the following week, I was given under that time to find sponsorship totalling £2,500. Working through the night I prepared a prospectus about the club and its event, setting off the next day in the direction of the venue; such was the reputation of both, that within forty eight hours I was able to head back ... cheques in hand.

Unfortunately the lot of the competitor or team is not easy as I am about to show:

i. The required amount for a seasons motorsport is likely to be far and away higher than that of the club or organiser.

ii. The approach to any prospective sponsor has to be more convincing and

The author's Lancia Lusso clearly exhibits the logos of product supporters, Avon Tyres, Castrol and NGK.

Clubman's ace John Istead gives value for money to a co-sponsor on the side-pods of his 1985 Mallock U2.

professional, remembering that it is not a right.

iii. The existence of the competitor or team in the 'hot-seat' will span only a comparatively short space of time when compared with the period of establishment of the average club or organiser.

iv. Competition for sponsorship amongst your fellows will be fierce and it is probable that you will come across many firms that have already been approached. Unfortunately, you will come across some who have become the victims of both disillusionment and maltreatment at the hands of your own and this will be something you'll have to learn to live with.

v. Sponsors will scrutinise you and your motives far more than they will a club, so that your appearance, your deportment and your display of humility will all help you to allay suspicions that all racing drivers are 'harum scarum' playboys or playgirls. Your first sponsor meeting could be traumatic: if you're young it will do you no harm to take Dad along, the sponsor will appreciate the gesture and Dad might just be able to stamp on your big foot before *you* put it in!

vi. Finally, satisfy yourself that you have something to offer by way of a few reasonable results, together with a few complimentary press mentions. Naturally, the more good results you have, the more sponsorship cash you are likely to command. If this puts off the novice I apologise, but facts are facts and the only practicable advice I can give these competitors is to get the 'wellie' in and get motoring! It only needs a bit of luck to reverse this situation; one, I may add, that we have all had to go through.

Your track record

You do not need to be Alain Prost, Team Lotus or even, at a slightly lower level, Maurizio Sandro Sala, but it will be to your advantage if at some time you've done something out of your own pocket, and that you are happy to continue doing so if all else fails. Do not listen to those who will tell you that anyone can get sponsored ... not true! You might be lucky, but by and large you'll need to show that you have what it takes, that is unless your father or mother has done it before you which, unfortunately, happens to be a fact of life for either the good or the bad. Get yourself the odd 'pot' or championship placing and your task will become that much easier; also you'll be in a far stronger position to put one across 'Ms. Worthington's daughter,' or son, in order to keep them both off the 'stage.' However, bear it in mind that there are many more competitors than there are clubs or interested organisers: it will take you much longer than forty eight hours to locate a sponsor, that is unless you're extremely lucky and despite your first class portfolio. Above all remember that you are not the only one chasing that all but illusive 'Utopia;' do not become disenchanted by your first refusal ... many more will follow I assure you.

Check list

i. Which of the following types of sponsorship will suit your purpose best:
Direct: for a championship, an event, a season, a series or simply a one-off event.
Product Support: if you are a club or organiser, this would be for advertising only. However, if you are an individual competitor or team, this could be for either advertising only or sponsorship, or both and will normally include the supply of accessories FOC as a part of the deal.
By Result: almost solely applicable to the individual competitor or team and is usually dependent upon your own plans, together with your competition affiliations. For example, if you drive an Opel or Vauxhall you might be tempted to try GM Dealership: an organisation that favours 'sponsorship by result.'
Underwritten: usually associated with the club or organiser and occasionally with the team seeking a form of financial insurance.
ii. Can you satisfy the eligibility 'stakes' by satisfying the following requirements?
iii. If you are a club or organiser, how long have you been established and what is your status (national etc.)?
iv. If you are a club or organiser, do you possess a sound record and, if so, what does this record consist of? Will it be as attractive to a sponsor as it is to your committee or to your management team?
v. If you are a club or organiser, are you sound both financially and by reputation.
vi. If you are an individual competitor or team, do you possess anything of a track record? Do you possess any wins or high placings? Do you almost invariably manage to finish? Do you have a reputation for good all-round sportsmanship?
vii. If you are an individual competitor or team, how long have you been competing and has it all been, to date, out of your own pocket? Will you carry on financing yourself, no matter how many sponsorship refusals you may get?
viii. Do the press view you favourably; even when you fail to gain a placing? Do the press mention you at all?
ix. Do you think that you are promotable?
x. Do you believe that your needs are honest and reasonable, and in keeping with your record?
xi. Are you capable of talking to higher management and if not, are you humble

enough to take along a mediator?

Competitors and Teams

If you can honestly answer 'yes' to at least 75% of your eligibility questions, then you have a good chance of reaching the negotiating table. Anything less and you could have a problem; get that placing and try again. Lastly, do try to avoid any approach which uses, or tries to use, the success of mother, father, brother or sister; the sponsor is only interested in you and what you have achieved!

Chapter 4

The Preliminary Research

Throughout the three previous Chapters I have recounted, briefly, the history and need for sponsorship, together with a review of the different types of support that are available and the eligibility requirements of all classes of candidate. In this Chapter I will begin to examine and explain the somewhat involved business of finding a sponsor.

I hope that most of you have read the preceding Chapters carefully, and that you will already appreciate that the emphasis is upon a planned approach to this challenge. However, no one in their right mind, either in a book or elsewhere, can justifiably claim that there is any magic formula for finding a sponsor; a state of affairs shared equally by the club, the competitor and the organiser. I am able to qualify that such a method of approach is essential by referring to my own, seemingly, successful sponsor hunts as having followed just such a path. Hence, as the title of this chapter implies, the necessity to embark upon a programme of research prior to all else is probably the most important aspect of the entire challenge.

In accord with Chapter three, it will be necessary for me to cover the same four subjects again: the club, the competitor, the organiser and the team, as follows:
Part 1. Preliminaries relating to the club or organiser.
Part 2. Preliminaries relating to the individual and team.
Part 3. Preliminaries relating to all candidates.
Part 4. Types of company likely to make good sponsor prospects.
Part 5. Types of company unlikely to make good sponsor prospects.

Part 1: Preliminaries relating to the club or organiser

Obviously the main item to be taken into consideration here is the eligibility of both candidates. However, in the case of the club this has already been dealt with in the second part of Chapter three. Referring to the organisers: whilst their eligibility has also been established, I feel that it is paramount that I describe briefly who such companies or people are likely to be.

An organiser will be an interested party of international, national or local repute that seeks to enhance their standing through an involvement in motorsport; examples being:

i. The company: The Daily express, former organisers of events like the 'International Trophy.'

ii. The person: Lord Montague of Beaulieu's many varied and interesting motoring spectaculars.

iii. The professional body: The British Racing Drivers Club; race organisers at Silverstone.

iv. The main sponsor: Lombard Banking, prestigeous promoters and part backers of the RAC Rally.

In conjunction with the establishment of their sponsorship eligibility, an organiser or club will, at the same time, decide upon the object behind their own particular sponsor hunt. This is likely to concern their interesting a prospective sponsor in one, or another, of the following:

i. A complete championship.

ii. A series of single events; for example, a combination consisting of a hillclimb, a race meeting, a rally and a sprint.

iii. A championship round.

iv. A one-off event.

Finally, the organiser may already be a main sponsor, like Lombard Banking, who seeks supporting finance for a big event. In this respect most firms of Lombard's standing should be able to rely, to some extent, upon their associates and clients in order that they might achieve this end.

Next in order of precedence will come the programme. Usually in the case of these candidates this should be available earlier than that of the individual or team. In many cases the programme could include championships or events that might require RAC/MSA approval, licensing or registration. Similarly, parts of the schedule may need to be co-ordinated in conjunction with other clubs or organisers. In consequence it is necessary for such parties to commence their quest for sponsorship and product support well in advance, and soon after having decided upon their seasonal plans. Most comprehensive and well supported calendars will have resulted from an advanced sponsorship programme often commenced well over a year before the opening date of the season in question. Many of you, like myself, will have at some time experienced the demoralisation that follows when a club or organiser has to cancel or suspend an event due to either bad timing, a lack of funds or a lack of support. A combination of any two of the latter factors will drop their reputation like the proverbial 'stone!' To any club or organising body that proposes a new sponsorship where time is of the essence, it is far better to seek out your 'supporting cast' sooner than later.

The sort of money that any sponsor candidate will require is of the utmost importance, as will be the budget which relates. In the case of the club or organiser, they will require a venue, they will require equipment, they will require the services and help of many people and, last, they will require a prize fund. All will need careful calculation offset against any contribution from their own funds, entry fees, and, where applicable, spectator charges. Much may need assessment, but whatever the result may be, it has to be as near to total accuracy as makes no difference. It will need a wealthy member to save the club if its figures are a mile out and likewise, it will be to the candidates' advantage to include a contingency of at least twenty percent to cover anything ·miscalculated or overlooked. Finally, do not make any reciprocal promises to your sponsor until you know that such is available and, above all, remember that it is in your interests to over-estimate rather than to find your club or company running short at the end of the day.

There are no hard and fast rules, but a number of clubs have told me that a budget guideline from their viewpoint might be:

i. £2,000 for a series of championship rounds being organised by a *national club*.

ii. £800 for an entire *county club* championship series.

iii. £350 for prizemoney and trophies relating to a *local club* event, or series.

In addition any status of club will be eligible for a reasonable advertising return from their programmes and entry regulations.

In the case of the organiser there are no guidelines; for one thing they may already be a main sponsor like Lombard Banking. On the other hand, their influence and reputation might command a few thousand if the event is big enough, whilst also enabling them to attract many independent advertisers not only to the pages of their programmes, but likewise to the venue, or venues, in question.

Choosing a sponsor will be important, and dependent upon the level of event, the candidate's requirement might from necessity involve either a reasonably large firm or merely a benevolent club member. Alternatively, if it is a national event the club or organiser might consider cash support by way of advertising someone's oil or sparking plugs. In this latter case be reasonable, many others could be seeking the same support and a hundred pounds or so from such a source is better than nought. The benefit which is offered to the sponsor will also play an important role in the candidate's ploy since, in this instance, it will be much easier for them to give both a continuing and stable return to their supporters than for any other status of participant. The events could be on-going, the funds should be readily negotiable if the sponsorship has been budgeted accurately and the venues will in most cases be well known, and repetitive. In addition one of the organising committee will almost certainly have been given the job of dealing with all the ensuing promotion and publicity, thereby establishing a distinct advantage over an individual competitor or team. Finally, the club will hold an annual dinner and prizegiving to which they normally invite their sponsors. In this event make sure that the appropriate press have been invited and include this item in your research programme.

Last, the venue. A matter, again, of prime consideration; it must be accessible, attractive, convenient and reasonably priced from a hirer's point of view. There should be a provision for all services: from those of an essential nature to those of a social function, refreshments and spectating fa-

cilities. For example, Oulton Park is a fine racing venue, but has little to offer the club or organiser using it for a speed-event series. Goodwood, on the other hand, has on offer a perpetual air display, a restaurant, superb scenery and usually fine weather, but like Oulton, discourages charging admittance to spectators. Brands Hatch and Doune have everything including shops, whilst offering an entirely different type of event: Brands Hatch specialising in racing and Doune in speed

hillclimbing. Consequently make sure that your venue has something to offer your sponsor and their clients. Likewise, you must take into account that it will be no use your programming an event at Goodwood because of its amenities if, say, your sponsor is based in Carlisle.

Part 2: Preliminaries relating to the individual competitor or team

I will assume that the candidates in this category have established their eligibility as good sponsor subjects. Therefore, I will move on to the somewhat obvious reason as to why you have deemed sponsorship to be necessary. Unless you fall into the multi-millionaire bracket there can be no

Stage participant Mike Kerr cornering his 2.3 litre Thompson Group Chevette, whilst displaying to good effect the consequences of an 'unsold' bonnet!

question of your going it alone, competitively, at Le Mans, whilst it is just as probable that you might not even complete a club championship without some kind of support. Similarly, if you've decided to indulge your engineering skills into producing a racing car and team then, again, you'll need substantial backing. It can in consequence be accepted that, having bought this book, you have long since decided why your own particular need requires you to find a sponsor.

Moving on to your programme and the timing of your approaches to your sponsor, the latter is more flexible in your case than in that of the club or organiser. For example, if you're about to design a car then you will have to know where the 'lolly' is coming from before you start. Conversely, if you require sponsorship for a one-off event in July then you might be able to leave your quest until April or May. There is nothing laid down and in the competitors case it is a matter of using one's discretion: I know of many drivers and teams that spend all their spare time seeking sponsors. Really it is a simple case of how much and when? There is however, one pitfall: sometimes the problem of when to start your hunt rests with the club or whosoever is running the event or series. Often diaries are late going to press, so that the rule here is not to wait until it is too late ... find out! Many a championship has been lost due to the participant waiting for dates and, in turn, losing the chance of sponsorship for it.

Yet another facet of the competitors research is the choice and preparation of the car or, in the case of a team, cars. This is an item of great priority, since no budget can be prepared by guesswork. It is a certainty that this will be the biggest item in your costings, so that it is a matter to be sorted out early on in your plans. Ask around and do not guess; it has been known for a participant to re-approach a sponsor in mid-season for more cash due to irresponsible planning. They might help,

but even if they do it will almost certainly spell the end of a beautiful friendship!

The type of company that you might approach is dictated by your eligibility. If, for example, you're into 'big time' rallying then you could try a firm like Martini & Rossi Ltd., whilst the same firm might also give you support on a smaller scale as has been my own experience. Should you wish to employ a guideline, it has to be that the status of company which you approach must reflect the status of yourself; the candidate, and the programme that you envisage. However, do not aim too high and don't be afraid to ask around. Even the motoring press will be only too happy to advise you of your worth, based upon your competition background and potential, the only issue in question being whether you are an amateur or professional and its bearing on your costings. Really the choice of sponsor is a matter for your conscience and it will be you who will have to convince the prospect that you are a worthy recipient. This will be dependent upon an honest appraisal of your own ability, or your team's, together with the costs you have arrived at.

Having sorted out the foregoing aspects of your research, now I will try to explain the level of sponsorship that our candidates might expect as follows:

i. **The competitor:** Imagine that you completed last season with a couple of class wins and a first six placing in a national or similar series. You could reasonably expect sponsorship to the value of £2,000, whilst also expecting a modicum of product support. However, should your first season have been as successful as Maurizio Sandro Sala's, then you might look forward to your request for 'ten grand' being favourably considered by the right firm. There is no hard and fast rule, but it has even been known for a poor season to be equally capable of producing Sala type sponsorship if the candidate has been seen as being promotable. By and large the better your track record, the more you should command.

ii. The team: Similar to the individual competitor. If you have nothing behind you: woe betide you. However, if your team just happens to include Alain Prost or a team manager named Fiorio then the sky could become the limit, more so if your team happens to be one that was included in last season's world championship placings.

If you are lucky your sponsor may be big enough to have a public relations department to look after your publicity return. If not, you will have to prepare just such a package yourself or alternatively, include an amount in your budget allocated to a PR agency or the like. Unfortunately many companies do not seem to favour the latter idea, so that it will be in your interest to assume this role yourself without being put upon. In any event it will do no harm for you to prepare your own promotional and publicity package even when your sponsor company does have available their own advertising or PR department.

The least important aspect of individual or team sponsorship research is that part of it which will examine the facilities that are available at event venues for the purpose of entertaining your sponsor and his clients. Unfortunately this is something over which neither party exercises much control; such amenities might or might not be available and moreover there could be a fee, so for goodness sake don't forget this. It is far more important for you to get your sponsor to be present at least three or four times per season, so that you must take into consideration that their representative will not take too kindly to being hauled from Carlisle, say, to Goodwood just to watch you. In other words spread your programme ... even if you don't like Ingliston.

In conclusion, evaluate your worth in terms of product and trade support. Your research should include your investigating the possibility of a little cash from these sources to offset against your car's maintenance. However, your list of product sponsors should, ideally, be restricted to six at the most: remembering that each one will want at least two adverts on your car.

Part 3: Preliminaries relating to all participants

Another important factor of this Chapter has to be finding out. The current periodical industry has a number of magazines available that may be ordered through the larger newsagent, who should also be able to show you a list. However, springing to mind are such journals as 'Boardroom', 'Campaign' and 'Marketing Week.' Akin to these are the business pages of the national dailys, local weeklys and, of course, the one and only 'Financial Times'. A little time spent perusing these papers can reveal all sorts of information including expansions, takeovers, data on new companies and new products. Take this information further and try to discover what you can about these firms, their operating areas, their products, the names of their senior executives and their press or public relations officer; if the latter exists.

Next I come to the hazard of the 'conflicting sport' and how this can affect every status of participant. When referring to this menace I am able to recount from a number of personal experiences. These show how this can create problems for the sponsor 'hunter.' Residing, at one time, in a part of South-Eastern England renowned for its 'horsey' activities, I found that almost every business had been approached, and in some cases frightened off, by a local and well known international venue. Likewise, the mother of almost every aspiring gymkhana competitor had been the rounds of all the smaller sources; hotels, pubs and shops. However, before I am accused of having a 'thing' about horses, I can assure you that it could equally be cricket, golf, tennis or even our own sport. Find out what goes on. It may not be obvious, but when you do come across a serious conflict look elsewhere; it will save you hours of frustration.

Part 4: The type of company likely to make good sponsor prospects

If you study our sport as precisely as I have done many things become clear, not least amongst them being the names of sponsors and the product or service each has to offer. When examined closer, it becomes even more obvious that these names fall into distinct categories to be seen over and over again, so that it makes sense to copy. Second, it can make a good talking point at any meeting or negotiating conference if you can relate to the success sponsorship has brought to similar firms and the competitor or participant involved.

There now follows a list of those types of company seen by me as offering the best sponsorship prospects to motorsport. Obviously there will be others, but those named should keep you busy for many a day:

Agricultural engineers. Anything new. Builders. Building Societies. Cigarette and Tobacco manufacturers. Civil engineers. Clothing manufacturers. Computer manufacturers. Computer centres. Computer hardware/software manufacturers. Cosmetics. Courier agencies. Dairy products. Development Boards. Drinks (alcoholic and non-alcoholic). Electrical engineers. Electronics. Employment agencies. Estate agents. Footwear manufacturers. Furniture manufacturers and shops. Hi-Fi equipment. Hotels. Hotel groups. Industrial bankers. Instant-Print groups. Insurance companies. Kitchen equipment. Medium-sized Car-Hire operators. Nationalised industries. Newspapers. Plant-Hire operators. Refrigeration manufacturers. Restaurant groups. Specialist services (Datapost etc.). Specialist travel. Technical and scientific equipment. Transport and allied services including shipping, but not airlines.

Part 5: The type of company unlikely to make good sponsor prospects

Just as there are those types of firm which make good prospects, there are, conversely, those which do not! What follows are a few all-round examples that can be qualified as time-wasters:

Airlines: They have their own outlets and are heavily into TV advertising.

The Aviation Industry: No connection with the world of motoring.

Brand Leaders: Some will and some will not! Very much a case of luck, but could be time consuming. Usually they rely largely upon magazine and TV advertising.

Car Manufacturers: Surprisingly they are generally hopeless, unless like General Motors and Toyota there is a department set aside, via their dealer network, for just such a purpose. A much changed and misunderstood scene: a matter that I could happily enlarge upon elsewhere!

Foreign Companies: Unless there is a specific connection, forget them.

Garages: They might finance an event, but generally they do not like spending money unless it is someone elses (for example, franchise promotion funds). When they can be persuaded to indulge, you can bet your life that they will expect a lot for a little.

Holiday Tour operators: In the main they are similar to the airlines.

International Car-Hire operators: I am not certain why such firms are loathe to become involved with motorsport sponsorship: possibly their American antecedents. Try Willhire or the like.

Leisure Groups: Inclined to favour the more energetic sports.

Music and Record Industry: Inclined to favour musical and other show business activities.

Shops: Some will, many won't.

Small Businesses: Nine times out of ten their owners are like the business; small minded.

32

By comparison with Mike Kerr's Chevette, the little Lancia Fulvia rally cars, as raced by the author, presented a disappointing frontal pose owing to their having a high bonnet line and lack of concave spoiler.

Television Advertisers: Either spent up or under an agent's thumb.

Check List

i. Satisfy yourself that you have an acceptable and eligible track record.

ii. Draw up a precise plan relating to your programme and keep to it.

iii. If you are a club or organiser, make sure that you are in possession of (ii) above in order that you have sufficient time to deal with the RAC/MSA, as well as the other items that follow. In your case it is more than likely that the original programme planning will be your responsibility.

iv. In the case of the individual competitor or team, it is essential that you have access to your proposed programme from the organiser(s) so that sufficient time is left for the remainder of your research and what follows.

v. If you are a club or organiser, select your helpers and your venues with an eye to cost.

vi. If you are an individual competitor or team, choose your car, or cars, early and investigate their preparation requirement.

vii. Investigate your own particular level of sponsorship whatever your status.

viii. Decide whether or not you will

require either product advertising or product support, dependant on your status.

ix. Select the size, status and type of firm to be approached and refer to marketing magazines, and newspapers as you deem necessary.

x. Prepare your budget with reasonable accuracy.

xi. If you are an individual competitor or team, select your venues with an eye to access, appeal, convenience and facility.

xii. Select your 'hunting' ground discriminately; taking into account all conflicting interests.

xiii. Find out the names of the relevant executives in the firms researched.

xiv. Find out if the firms selected employ either their own advertising or public relations staff and plan accordingly.

Chapter 5

Preparing your Approach

Having dealt adequately with the question of sponsorship research, now I come to that part of the search for a sponsor when, all things being equal, we embark upon the task of preparing all the data accumulated. In this respect I am sure that my readers will appreciate, as this chapter unfolds, the wisdom behind the thoroughness that I have advised throughout the foregoing text.

Before settling down to the question of 'preparing the approach,' this is probably as good a place as any for me to make a somewhat small, but nevertheless important point. What I am about to describe is the method of preparing oneself, in whatever capacity, to go out and obtain the necessary support be it large, mediocre or merely a few litres of oil. May I respectfully make it clear that although the three types of approach have worked many times for myself, someone else may find that an alteration or modification might suit their own ideas and requirements that much better. Obviously the candidates are free to adapt my practice as they see fit. Likewise, I would be very foolish to imply that this book offers any guarantee: suffice to say that it has worked for me, not once but many times. I will however, agree that salesmanship does play an important part, but equally so does determination!

In this Chapter I will be describing three differing plans:

Plan A: to be adopted when approaching a prospective sponsor for a single event sponsorship or for nominal support.
Plan B: to be adopted when seeking either product support or advertising sponsorship.
Plan C: to be adopted when planning the way to approach a main sponsor.

Plan A: Preparing the approach for nominal or event sponsorship

Believing very much in the wisdom of simplicity, the rules of this particular 'game' are easy to follow and apply to any status of candidate. Assuming that the latter is a club seeking £350 for a one day national sprint at Goodwood, it will be accepted that the organisation in question has been in existence for some time during which a reasonable reputation has been acquired both in competition spheres and in club circles. Therefore, there is no question of their eligibility, since this has already been established.

Referring to the previous Chapter we will assume that the club has selected Goodwood due to its having very few conflicting interests and none which account for a great deal in the way of sponsorship other than, perhaps, horse racing. Having budgeted as accurately as makes no difference, the committee have opted for a nominal sponsor to cover a deficit totalling £350. They require the sponsorship cash to be made available prior to the event and have agreed, provisionally, that any residue will be returned. A condition being that the sponsor utilises any such sum for their own publicity in conjunction with the event.

Supposing that the event is scheduled for the month of June, your planning must start very early in the New Year. First, in your list of priorities, is the selection of at least ten prospective sponsors. Why ten? Experience has led me to believe that this number has a good chance of producing three replies and at least one negotiation. Finding this number can be achieved by visiting the local chamber of trade, the local industrial estates and by examining the local press. The first should be able to provide details concerning firms which have recently moved into the area, together with any information regarding those that are manufacturing new products, whilst likewise, time can be well spent talking to the business editor of the largest local newspaper. However, any information gleaned should be in the hands of the club's committee leaving at least four months to cover the approach, the negotiation and the finalisation of any deal.

The committee having settled upon a number of reliable firms may then, at their discretion, either phone or write to each. In this respect I have always been an advocate of the written word for two reasons:

i. It only costs a **first class** stamp.

ii. You are giving the prospective sponsor something to chew over, providing your letter says sufficient to whet the appetite. No doubt you will have observed the emphasis upon 'first class' postage: never send such a letter by any other means ... it shows a mean streak and it may have little or no chance of by-passing an astute secretary. Alternatively, should you decide to telephone: always confirm such an approach in writing and never commit anything to memory. It is also essential that your correspondence should be addressed to an individual and marked 'personal'.

Any letter, even if only a confirmation must follow a formula that gives brief information about the club, the event, the finance being sought and the publicity being offered. All the letters must be typed on official notepaper and should, if at all possible, be posted at one and the same time and not less than three months prior to the event's scheduled date: in so doing you may encourage the theory of concurrent and speedy replies. Finally, try and heed my advice concerning a written approach, it will save you pounds and also a great deal of frustration, since it is almost certain that your prospect will have lost the hastily scribbled note giving your phone number! For guidance only, the appendix to this section, which can be found at the end of this Chapter, contains an example of such a letter, which has been found by me to be quite adequate in the past.

Plan B: Preparing the approach to a product sponsor

Elementary in practice, we will accept that the 'hunter' is the well established, but ficticious 'United Banking Group' who are the main sponsors of the similarly ficticious 'United National Stage Rally Championship.' This series consists of eight rounds and 'United' having put up 75% of the sponsorship required, still need the remaining 25% by way of product support as follows:

i. 7% to cover the fuel expenses for the rally officials.

ii. 6% for the printing of road-books in respect of all eight rounds.

iii. 5% for the provision of scrutineering premises for all eight rounds.

iv. 5% to cover the officials' and organisers' accommodation at all eight venues.

v. 2% for press hand-outs.

''United' now seek five firms for the purposes stated.

Now I come to the nitty-gritty. Do not imagine for one minute that just because you're the co-ordinator of 'United Banking's' motorsporting interests that your troubles will be few. You may well be involved with one of Europe's major banking groups, but alas, there is more to it than that and in the context of Chapters three and four: you will still have to do your homework and to get your research right! For example, there is no use your approaching 'Newtown Car Accessories' if Newtown is only representative of one round in the series. Likewise, should you think of approaching a firm like ICI's Automotive Division, they are likely to tell you that they prefer Keke Rosberg since he participates in international events, whilst your series only attracts national interest.

The ideal basis on which to start is the fact that your series is of national status. This in itself will open the door to almost every large motoring orientated organisation, in addition to other nationals. However, there is still much to be done even at this stage, and next you will need to decide the amount of advertising space that you are going to make available to each of the five interested sponsors. When referring to this publicity return, 'United' may consider apportioning this as follows:

Fuel expenses: advertising on all rally cars and support vehicles.

Road-books: advertising within, or on, the covers of books, as well as a display on the rally car decals.

Scrutineering premises: advertising on all support caravans, hospitality units and official vehicles.

Officials' and organisers' accommodation: advertising at all eight rally headquarters, as well as at every forest stage.

Press hand-outs: advertising in all the pre and post event press coverage where possible and in the hand-outs themselves.

Now I come to the million dollar question, what types of firm to approach? First of all you'll need to cover yourself by making at least thirty approaches in order to produce five successful results, whilst remembering that the rallying season spans the entire year so that your approaches should commence at least six months prior to the date of the first round. In this instance I would choose six firms from each of the following categories:

Fuel: any six petroleum companies.

Scrutineering: any six national transport concerns of all types, but preferably road transport.

Road-Books: the general press, magazine publishers, motoring publishers and the national motoring press.

Accommodation: national hotel groups and especially those with hotels that are convenient to the eight rally headquarters.

Hand-Outs: any six national accessory groups.

In every case the approach should be made in writing unless the series is on-going. Enclose with the letter details of each round and include the names of any well known competitors that you expect to enter together with the details of 'United's' own financial involvement as the main sponsor. Last, make it clear why the sum is required and when the cash will be needed; usually a well advanced date. Any negotiation will have to agree who pays for the relevant advertising material: banners, decals and printed matter. This question should be settled at the outset and included in your costs, since it can be one that might cost you dearly. Preferably this should be down to the supporter, but should there be any doubt add on a reasonable sum to cover same. Once again it is much better to over-estimate than to have to go back again for more; in which event you run the risk of becoming the recipient of the 'Oliver Twist' treatment in addition to a substantial loss of face.

When considering the approach letters and the distribution of these: they should be posted together and, again, by first class postage following the guidelines of plan 'A'. However, do not forget to enclose a full specification of the publicity return you are offering in each case. An example of this return along with the relevant letter can be found by referring to appendix 'B' at the end of this Chapter.

Plan C: Preparing the approach to a main sponsor

My readers will appreciate that attempting to raise a substantial sum of money for any venture, business or otherwise, is dependent upon how well one convinces a prospective backer as to the scheme's viability, should it be the former or its worthiness, should it be the latter. Doubtless many of you may have considered investing in shares and as a result will have received via your bankers, or stockbroker, one of those glossy folders telling you about the firm and its future prospects, supported by its latest balance sheet. This publication is commonly known as a 'prospectus,' a similar work being on offer by schools anxious to persuade the enquiring parent that one establishment is better than another. Consequently, when it comes to either an individual competitor or a team contemplating a hunt for any sum which exceeds a few hundred pounds, the recognised method of setting about the task is for the candidate to produce a comprehensive prospectus which will give details of their record to date, their plans and their prospects. This, it is hoped, should serve to convince the prospective sponsor that their investment will be cost effective, properly administered and worthwhile. It can also be said that the more professional one makes one's prospectus look, the more successful your approach is likely to be. There is however, a proviso that the candidate has observed the 'rules of play' outlined in Chapters three and four, and that he, or she, has complied with these rules to the letter.

Since the main content of this plan centres around the competitor's pros-pectus and its production, I will commence my description of how to go about the latter by listing the results of a **known** candidate's preliminary research, as follows:

i. The candidate is female and races in Formula Ford 1600.

ii. It is her third season and she has completed her previous two with an outright win in a newcomers' championship, a second in another championship, a fourth in another and a fifth in yet another. The foregoing results also include several individual high class positions and overall placings.

iii. She possesses a national racing licence and owns the car, which is to be updated for the coming season.

iv. She has carefully, and with advice, prepared a sound budget: the level of sponsorship being sought is average for both her ability and her plans.

v. She requires sponsorship from a moderately sized national company and is not concerned with any conflicting sports, although such is considerable where she lives and, ironically, comes from the same sport. She will be competing at national level and so is able to negotiate sponsorship nationwide.

vi. She has completed all her necessary preliminaries by November, with her first scheduled event being in early March.

vii. She is aged in her late twenties and is by profession a management consultant employed by the BBC.

From the foregoing, readers will observe that the candidate is not only eligible and promotable, but that she has also taken care of all the preliminaries meticulously. At this point I will tell you that my subject is factual and is, by name, Miss Antonia Loysen. I would also like to say how much I appreciate the help that she has given to me with this part of Chapter five, which includes the authority for me to use her own 1983 prospectus. However, it should be noted that whilst the example I have chosen is a female, the same applies to the male competitor or team.

Dealing first with the layout of the prospectus, this follows a set sequence which can be examined by referring to Antonia's prospectus which immediately follows this Chapter and which is detailed below:

i. A card cover usually size A4 on which should appear the name of the candidate, their motoring interest, their future plans, the championships or premier awards held and the events to be contested. In this respect Antonia has kept her own cover brief, as can be seen; I personally would have said a little more as suggested.

ii. A brief personal background.

iii. Your track record.

iv. Details and specification of your car, or cars.

v. Your proposed programme with map and venues.

vi. Your budget in detail.

vii. The promotion and publicity return you are offering.

viii. Three pages of selected, and recent, press cuttings.

The entire presentation should be interspersed with at least six black and white photographs of the driver or team in action. In the case of an individual competitor there should also be a recent self-portrait, whilst in the case of a team there should be a recent photograph of the entire crew: suitably identifying the drivers, team manager and chief mechanic.

The making-up of the prospectus is usually done from a 'master' copy that contains all the candidate's original material. Everything should be typed accurately and similarly, the map which shows your proposed venues must again be neatly and properly drawn, with the intended photographs and press cuttings mounted on card and labelled accordingly. The next step, having put the 'master' together as indicated, is to find a good photocopying establishment that can reproduce not only the text, but the photographs as well. By this process produce six copies of the complete 'master' including six *original* descriptive covers (these should not be copies), so that the finished articles give the appearance of being a wholly professional job. It is also a good idea to find someone locally who is able to heat-bind: this inexpensive process usually incorporates a clear PVC cover and can be obtained at certain instant printing shops in the Prontaprint group.

Apart from the time and trouble well spent on collating and typing, the only costs involved in producing six copies will be the photocopying and binding. However, please note that the typescript must be neat and should not be attempted if this function is not amongst the candidate's own talents. In such an event, do not hesitate to find someone who will undertake this work for you. A few pounds invested in an able copy typist won't go amiss and the finished result will certainly look better than haphazard spacing, misspelling and two gallons of typist's correcting fluid!

Whilst on the subject of professionalism, if it is a particularly big sponsorship which is being sought, invest in the services of a graphic artist who will depict the car and your overalls in the livery of any prospective sponsor. This can be quite impressive, but will require six colour facsimiles which might pose a problem unless you happen to reside near one of our bigger commercial towns.

Why a prospectus at all, why six copies and why specifically should they be produced on A4 paper? First, a prospectus is more likely to create an interest and will enable the candidate to get away with a brief covering letter. Second, six copies allows the candidate to cover a lot of ground quickly. Third, A4 has become the basic size of the current business communication, whilst also being a convenient size and inexpensive to post. The cost of production comes next and this can vary from a nominal £15 for half a dozen to a couple of hundred pounds, dependent on how professional you want the end product to be. Whatever the cost, remember to enclose the requisite postage stamps for the prospectus to be returned and *never* send, or leave, your 'master' under any circumstances. This is most important, since the loss of this will be, at the very least, catastrophic.

In several parts of this Chapter reference has been made to the use of headed notepaper. This is seen by most candidates as being something of a MUST and although readily available to the club or organiser, it might not be available to the individual or team. Call yourself, for example, 'John Smith Racing' and prepare a neat display showing your address, championships held, important results, together with your telephone number. Single or double colour should suffice. This will come within the scope of any commercial printer. However, if you really are after the 'big time' and have money to burn then, again, any graphic artist will design such a layout for you. In any event, and whatever your decision, avoid writing to any status of prospective sponsor on unheaded paper.

In conclusion, it will do no harm for the candidates from all four categories to announce their intentions and requirements to the motoring press and other media outlets in a press release per the examples shown in the specimen which follows:

A club press-release

The Home-Counties Car Club intend to organise a national sprint meeting at Goodwood during 1986. With their plans well advanced, the Club's chairman states that a comprehensive sponsor search is now well in hand with a view to finding a company willing to support and underwrite the finance required for their ambitious venture. The club invite any interested party to contact the secretary on 01.100.1000 for further details.

An organisers press-release

United Banking once again announce their sponsorship of the 1986 'United National Stage Rally Championship'. The contest will consist of eight rounds commencing with the Welsh in February and finishing with the Irish in November. United are anxious to attract five additional sponsors willing to substantiate their own confirmed 75% backing. Interested parties are assured of comprehensive publicity from the series, and should contact the United co-ordinator on 01.100.1000 for further details.

An individual competitors press-release

Antonia Loysen, the Silverstone based Formula Ford driver, has recently announced her plans to continue in this category during the coming season. Once again at the wheel of a Royale RP26, Miss Loysen will be contesting the Esso Formula Ford Championship and the BWRDC's Goodwin Trophy, as last year. Sponsorship of an average amount is being sought, and with just two and a half months to her first round any interested party should contact the driver on Silverstone (0327) 100000 for details.

Check list

i. Formulate your approach plans well in advance.

ii. Select your championship, series or venue, ensuring that your choice offers all-round sponsor appeal.

iii. Should you be a club or organiser selecting a venue, guard against conflicting sporting interests.

iv. Decide upon the type and level of sponsorship that will suit your own particular needs best.

v. Consult all sources of local information that are relevant to your own particular participation.

vi. Ensure, at this stage, that you have left no stone unturned.

vii. From the information at your disposal, select ten possible prospects and in turn research the entire 'modus operandi' of each one.

viii. Decide when you will require your sponsorship funds to be made available, so that this can be included in your approach and/or prospectus.

ix. Decide whether or not you should phone first or write, but remember, above all, that your first aim must be to convince your prospect that your cause is worthwhile. From my own point of view I prefer to write in the first instance.

x. Should you decide to phone first, don't forget to confirm any productive conversation in writing.

xi. Any participant can use a prospectus to highlight their proposals. In this respect, this is the stage when you should set about producing same so that this item can accompany your first written communication.

xii. Always use headed notepaper. If you are an individual or team, give yourself a name; for example, 'John Smith Racing.'

xiii. Always use first class postage and always enclose the requisite stamps for the return of your prospectus, where this is applicable.

xiv. Post all your first contact letters together. This might encourage concurrent replies.

xv. When producing your prospectus, do not forget the all-important issue of who is going to pay for all the very necessary advertising material? Similarly, do not forget this issue even if your particular approach does not include a prospectus.

xvi. Announce the finalisation of your plans to the press by way of a simple release.

The Prospectus

i. Observe the rules of composition that are detailed in the text.

ii. Do not attempt to produce your prospectus without help; there is nothing worse than something of importance which sparks of DIY. Likewise, if you can't type ... then don't.

iii. If your needs are substantial, do not hesitate to use the services of a graphic artist; money well spent.

iv. Always produce a minimum of six. I have found from experience that this allows me to obtain the maximum coverage in the shortest possible time.

v. Never give away your 'master' and always enclose sufficient stamps for its return.

ANTONIA LOYSEN RACES

FORMULA FORD 1600

1983

ANTONIA LOYSEN

ADDRESS

109 Fentiman Road, Vauxhall, London SW8 1JZ.
Telephone: 01- 735 5087

Soon moving to Silverstone.

AGE

28

OCCUPATION

Management Consultant
Breakfast Television, B.B.C.

EDUCATION

Uplands School, Poole, Dorset.
University College London.
(B.Sc. Hons in Mathematics)

RACING AWARDS

BWRDC Jean Denton Newcomers Trophy 1981
2nd BWRDC Helen Spence Trophy 1981
5th BWRDC Goodwin Trophy 1981

Pre-57 Saloon Car Championships 1981:
Road-going   4th in class
                  9th overall
Modified   2nd in Class
                  6th overall

11th COMCC Racing Championship 1981

Currently 4th in 1982 BWRDC Championship

HOBBIES

Singing - member of Tadige Singers (an octet
who have given numerous performances in London
and the Home Counties of programmes ranging
from sixteenth century church music to close
harmony arrangements of popular songs).

Squash - Captain of UCL Ladies Squash Team and
currently member of two South London Clubs.

Hockey - member of Dorset Junior Hockey Team
and several clubs since then. Captain of Barnes
2nd XI Ladies Hockey Team in 1979/80.
(Retired at present due to lack of time).

Old Citroëns - especially the "Traction Avant"
Light 15 or Maigret car. Archivist for the
Traction Owners Club.

1983

ESSO FF1600 CHAMPIONSHIP DATES

Sunday 6th March	Silverstone
Sunday 13th March	Thruxton
Weekend 19th/20th March	Silverstone
Monday 4th April	Silverstone
Monday 2nd May	Silverstone
Saturday 7th May	Silverstone
Monday 30th May	Silverstone
Saturday 4th June	Snetterton
Weekend 11th/12th June	Silverstone
Sunday 10th July	Brands Hatch
Sunday 24th July	Donnington
Sunday 6th August	Oulton Park
Monday 29th August	Silverstone
Weekend 10th/11th September	Silverstone
Weekend 1st/2nd October	Silverstone

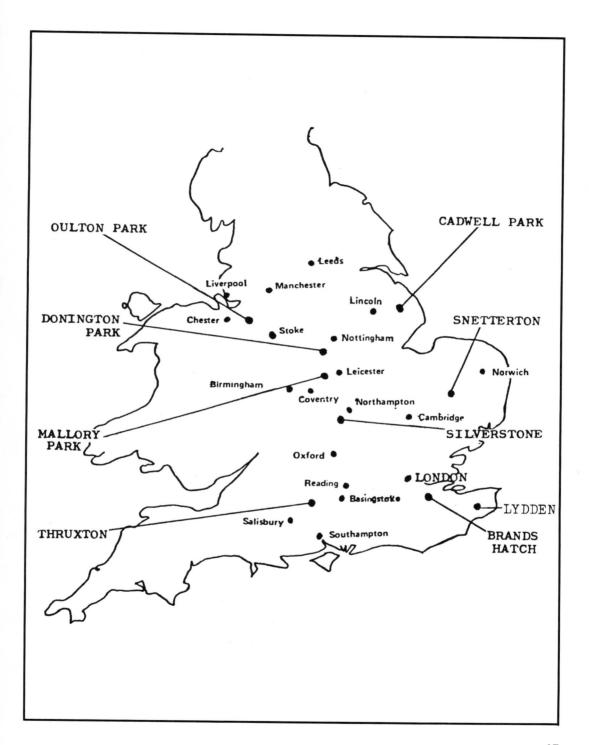

OULTON PARK

CADWELL PARK

Leeds

Liverpool   Manchester

Lincoln

DONINGTON
PARK

Chester   Stoke

Nottingham

SNETTERTON

Birmingham   Leicester

Norwich

Coventry   Northampton

Cambridge

MALLORY
PARK

SILVERSTONE

Oxford

Reading

LONDON

Basingstoke

LYDDEN

THRUXTON

Salisbury

Southampton

BRANDS
HATCH

45

Formula Ford 1600

Costs

1983

	£ per mile
Engine rebuild (£500 every 500 miles)	1.00
Petrol at 15 mpg	.11
Oil (1 can per 500 miles)	.01
Plugs (1 set per 500 miles)	.01
Brakes (£20 per 500 miles)	.05
Tyres (£207 per 500 miles)	.41
Running cost per mile	1.59

Cost per test session	£	£
100 miles at £1.59	159.00	
Session fee	25.00	
Mechanic (setting up and test session)	75.00	
		259.00
Cost per race		
40 miles at £1.59 (practice + race)	63.60	
Race entry	30.00	
Mechanic	50.00	
		143.60
Cost for race and test		402.60

Additional Costs

1. Entrants Licence.

2. Advertising permit.

3. New bodywork for racing car:

    New nosecone plus spare (cost new approx £90.00 + vat)
    Both side panels (probably available second hand
                        new cost is approx £125.00 + vat each)
    Top body panel (probably available second hand)

4. Painting and signwriting racing car.

5. Painting and signwriting van.

6. Petrol to circuit.

7. Overnight accomodation at circuits away from Silverstone.

8. Crash damage repairs. Could be anywhere between £1,000 and £2,000.
    (Hopefully not more)

Guestimates for above costs

	For 10 races	for 17 races
1 to 5	£ 700.00	£ 700.00
6	£ 50.00	£ 85.00
7	–	£ 100.00
8	£1000.00	£1700.00
	1750.00	2585.00

Additional costs per race are about £163.00
Making total cost of sponsoring for the season, as £565.00 per race

MOTOR RACING
EXCITING AND EYECATCHING

Have you ever thought of using a racing car to give you more widespread and exciting publicity?

There are various ways in which a fast 120 mile-an-hour single seater racing car can be used to promote your company's image.

ADVERTISING AT THE CIRCUIT

Company X Ltd. on the side of the car.
Company X Ltd. in the programme as the entrant.
Company X Ltd. written on the car transporter.
Company X Ltd. written on Tee-shirts and overalls worn by the team.
Stickers and badges can be produced and distributed at circuits.
Hospitality suites can be hired and demonstrations arranged at circuits to entertain Company X Ltd's customers while races are being run. It impresses customers to meet THEIR driver.

PUBLICITY IN THE MEDIA

Although it is not a new thing in motor racing, I have an additional pull in the media over other drivers by being a girl!

I am the only girl competing regularly in FF1600 at a national level, and with Desire Wilson (the only girl to have won a Formula One race) off to America, I might soon find myself as the fastest lady racing driver in the U.K.

I am hoping to be involved in a programme by TV South on Women in Motor Sport. I have also been promised an item on the BBC Breakfast television when that begins early next year.

At least one of the races I am entering will be televised and I am hoping to arrange some radio interviews nearer the end of the season. I will be racing in one of the supporting races at the only non-championship Grand Prix race which will be held at Donington Park at the end of the season.

EXHIBITIONS AND TRADE SHOWS

The car can be used as part of an eyecatching display on a stand at an exhibition.

A video tape of races could be made and shown on a trade stand. This always draws a crowd.

COMPETITIONS

Motor racing can be linked into staff or customer competitions. For example, Rizzla who sponsor a Formula Three car and a Grand Prix car, have a competition to send the winner to a Grand Prix next year.

THRUXTON

Antonia in number 10 outbraking number 23 into the chicane on the last lap of the race, to cross the line 0.8 seconds ahead of him!
(He got his revenge a couple of weeks later by pushing me off at Silverstone)

Tel: 0273.123456

June Laird Racing

1984 HSCC Speed-Events Champion
1982 & '83 BWRDC National Hillclimb Champion
1983 BARC National Lady Hillclimb Champion
1983 BARC/PACE National Sprint Championship
Class Winner
1982 BARC (L & HCC) Ladies Champion
1985 BARC Halliday Trophy
Holder of Ten Outright Land-Speed Records
(Class 'E' 1600-2000cc)

The Sales and Marketing Director,
Harringtons Ltd.,
Old Shoreham Road,
<u>HOVE</u>
East Sussex.   West Sussex

<u>Personal</u>   14th July '85

Dear Sir,

You will see from the attached photograph and the enclosed
prospectus that I am one of a handful of successful lady
racing drivers, a land speed record holder and recipient of
numerous prestigeous championship firsts.

Specialising in the 'historic' category of motorsport, I have
recently acquired a race modified Honda S.800 Coupe which I
intend to use at national level between now and the seasons
end.

Well connected with the local press throughout Sussex as
well as with some nationals, together with Radio Brighton
and TVS I am able to offer a professional publicity deal
in return for sponsorship which is detailed in the enclosed
prospectus.

Residing locally, I am able to discuss my plans with you
at your convenience should you find my track record whets
your appetite.

Yours sincerely,

June Laird.

Appendix 'A' See over.

Whilst the name and address of the firm shown in the following 'Appendix A' is factual: the BARC address, contents and signatory are ficticious.

The British Automobile Racing Club's London Centre notepaper has been used for effect and in this respect the author wishes to express her gratitude to the Centre's former editor for the supply of same for the purpose stated.

BRITISH AUTOMOBILE RACING CLUB

LONDON AND HOME COUNTIES CENTRE
(INCORPORATING SURREY NORTH THAMES & S.E. CENTRES)

R.T. Ward Esq.,
Lucas-Girling Ltd.,
Birmingham Road,
West Bromwich,
West Midlands.

Please reply to   The Comps Sec'y,
Queens Court,
Kingsville,
Princetown.

28th Dec. 1984

Dear Sir,

You will be well acquainted with the above organisation
and its indisputable record in the field of motorsport.

The above Centre are this coming year organising a one
day NATIONAL sprint meeting at Goodwood during July. At
present the provisional date is the 21st.

The committee have authorised me to approach your firm
with a request for event support in return for venue
and other allied advertising relevant to the event. The
sum sought is a maximum of £350 by way of an underwritten undertaking. The sponsorship is required by the
31st of May, 1985 with any residue being repaid to your
company for the purpose of your publcising the event.

Should you be interested, the writer will be pleased to
either discuss in person or to forward further details.
and in closing would add that the sprint would be known
as the Lucas-Girling BARC (LHCC) National Sprint.

Yours sincerely,

John Smith.

Competitions Secretary

APPENDIX A

BRITISH AUTOMOBILE RACING CLUB

LONDON AND HOME COUNTIES CENTRE
(INCORPORATING SURREY, NORTH THAMES & S.E. CENTRES)

Please reply to BARC (LHCC)

Princetown.

Sponsorship return Goodwood sprint

Lucas-Girling Ltd.,
West Bromwich.   28th Dec. 1985

In return for the sponsorship suggested, the BARC (LHCC) will
undertake the promotion of Lucas-Girling as follows:

The event will be known and publicised as the Lucas-Girling
national sprint.
This title will be shown on all entry forms, final regulations
and rsults. This title will be the subject of a formal BARC/
Lucas-Girling agreement.
Banners displaying Lucas-Girling will be displayed at the venue
in accordance with Goodwood Terrena guidelines.
All competing cars and support vehicles will display Lucas-Girling
decals prior to the event.

Advertising banners and decals will be supplied by Lucas-Girling;
the BARC (LHCC) being responsible for all other advertising and
printing.

The BARC (LHCC) will appoint a publicity officer who will be
responsible for handling all the media publicity in relation to
the event.

pp. The committee, BARC (LHCC).

APPENDIX B

UNITED BANKING PLC
Fenchurch Street
London EC
01.100.1000

The Publicity and Marketing Director,
The County Hotels Group,
Western Road,
Oldtown,
Midlandshire.

Our Ref: JS/MS   30th Sept. 1985

Dear Mr. Jones,

Re-The 1986 United National Stage Rally Championship

Once again United Banking will be sponsoring the eight rounds of the prestigious rally championship detailed above. The eight events are each based in Newtown: Mid-Wales, Chester, Durham, Kendal in Cumbria, Dumfries in Scotland, Nottingham, Reading and Antrim: N. Ireland.

Attracting at least 100 competitors per round, we envisage – as last year – entries from such well known participants as Russell Brookes, Steve King, Tony Pond and representing the ladies, Louise Aitken-Walker and Michele Mouton.

United's part of the total sponsorship is 75% or £18,000 from a requirement of £24,000. Since County Hotels have a hostelry at each one of our eight venues, we would like to interest your company in a 5% part sponsorship totalling £1200 to cover the accommodation for the rally officials. Should you be interested in assisting us in this way, County Hotels will receive publicity per the attached schedule throughout the currency of the series.

The undersigned will gladly travel to Oldtown at your convenience to discuss this matter further.

Yours sincerely,

John Smith, Rally Co-ordinator for United Banking PLC.

APPENDIX B

UNITED BANKING PLC
Fenchurch Street
London EC
01.100.1000

The County Hotels Group,
Western Road,
Oldtown,
Midlandshire.

Our Ref: JS/MS   30th Sept. 1985

Sponsorship Return United National Stage Rally Championship

In return for the sponsorship suggested, United Banking will undertake the promotion of County Hotels as follows:

County Hotels will be publicised and displayed at every one of the forest stages that form the nucleus of the eight round series.

County Hotels will be publicised and displayed at each one of the eight rally headquarters nationwide.

The liaison will be announced to the motoring press, the national press, local radio and television as applicable to each of the venues.

The publicity displays at each forest stage and rally HQ will comprise banners and advertising signs which are to be provided by County Hotels. Any other form of press or publicity release to be provided at the expense of United Banking PLC.

United Banking will be further responsible for the administration of any relevant publicity via our press officer, yet to be appointed.

pp. United Banking PLC

APPENDIX C

01.973.1000   **JOHN SMITH RACING**

Holders of numerous prestigious motor
racing championship firsts and seconds

Drivers: John Smith and Mary Smith

The Competitions Director,   "Monza,"
Lucas-Girling Ltd.,   Grosvenor Place,
Birmingham Road,   London NE2.4WX
West Bromwich
West Midlands B71.4JR   1st Jan'y 1985

Dear Mr. Green,

As you will see from the letterhead we are a racing team of considerable track record presently competing in both circuit racing and speed events.

Car-wise we compete in Clubman's with a Mallock U2, and in speed events with a VW Golf GTI. Photographs herewith.

One of the hazards of motorsport especially speed eventing, is the fact that ones brakes, although disc, seem particularly susceptible to a high degree of wear necessitating regular replacement. In this respect the system is by origin "Girling."

In the same way that we receive support from such companies as Avon, Castrol, Koni and NGK, the team are wondering if you would be prepared to supply the necessary pads, details to follow, plus, say £250, towards our seasonal costs. In return for such a gesture we would be happy to provide the publicity return appended hereto.

Looking forward to the favour of your early reply, our season commences late March.

Yours sincerely,

pp. John Smith Racing,

John Smith, Principal   *Ficticious*

Encl: Publicity Return and Photographs (2).

APPENDIX C

01.973.1000   JOHN SMITH RACING

The Competitions Director,
Lucas-Girling Ltd.

Publicity and Promotion Return 1985   1st Jan'y 1985

In return for the nominal sponsorship sought plus product support by way of FOC disc pads, John Smith Racing will be pleased to confirm a publicity package as follows:-
i. To display Lucas-Girling decals on both cars throughout the season at the rate of four per vehicle.
ii. To display similar on our transporter vehicle.
iii. To display Lucas-Girling badges in such a non-conflicting place that can be found on the team's overalls.
iv. To announce our union in the major motorsporting press.
v. To detail such a union in all commentary notes.
vi. To distribute, as requested, any literature publicising Lucas-Girling products.
vii. To undertake at least one event with yourselves as Entrant for programme publicity purposes.
viii. To use at all times Lucas-Girling pads and linings as well as the appropriate fluids etc.

Finally, we would confirm that the supply of the necessary decals shall be the responsibility of Lucas-Girling along with any relevant publicity data. John Smith Racing will furthermore agree to your being kept informed of the teams results on a week by week basis.

The prospect may before finalisation add or subtract any clause that they deem fit after consultation with the team.

pp. John Smith Racing,

John Smith, Principal

Ficticious

Lucas

APPENDIX C2

Lucas Batteries Limited
Formans Road
Sparkhill
Birmingham B11 3DA

Telephone: 021-777 3292
Telex: 338651

Mrs June Laird

ADE/SMU
8 February 1984

Dear Mrs Laird

Thank you for your letter dated 6 February 1984.

I am sorry for our failure to reply to your previous letter, but rest assured neither it, nor its contents were ignored.

A non standard battery is currently being assembled, within our laboratory, which will have the same physical dimensions as type 077, but will have a higher performance level.

It is anticipated that this battery will be available within the next 7 to 10 days and you will be advised accordingly.

I am enclosing a selection of labels which I trust will prove useful in advertising the Lucas name and hope that this information proves satisfactory .   I will be writing again shortly.

Yours sincerely

R W WARD
Marketing & National Accounts Manager

Encl:

Registered office Well Street Birmingham B19 2XF Registered no.256789 London

Chapter 6

Approaching a Prospective Sponsor and Negotiating a Sponsorship

I would like to recount part of 'Plan A', Chapter five. In the example used the club were looking for a sponsorship assessed at £350 and having decided upon a suitable selection of sponsor prospects the question is, should they telephone or should they write? Presuming that the club is well known and their prospect local, a senior committee member should, in this instance, telephone the firm concerned asking to speak with the relevant executive ... in person. When making such a call do not presume that your contact knows all about you, but assume that he, or she, does not; therefore, introduce yourself and your club in as few words as practicable. Follow this up with a brief resume about your request, stating that you have been 'asked' to send details of the event to a number of local business houses and that you would like to include them in the club's circulation. Whilst this strategy is something of a ploy, it usually works and will tend to temper what otherwise might end up as a non-productive question and answer session. Leave your conversation at that, but follow it up with a letter, as soon as possible, enclosing the club's publicity return as shown in appendix A, Chapter five. The prospective sponsor's reply might take one of four forms: straightforward no!, a request for more details, an invitation to discuss your proposition or a 'yes', by way of an agreement or cheque in the post. In the latter case, surprising as it may seem, it has often been known for the sum requested to simply appear in this way.

At this stage it might be advantageous if I deal with the question so often asked by sponsor prospects, why motorsport? In such an event 'be prepared,' and when writing, support your telephoned conversation with a copy of the specimen answer, which you will find in appendix D, this Chapter. Second, even though the sum sought may seem modest, treat your prospect as you would if it were a million and remember that **they** are more interested in what they hope to receive, than in what they might be going to give to you.

Whatever the reply, with the exception of a 'no', confirm this in writing by return and from then on keep your prospect well informed, especially if the event is some time off. Likewise, make it clear just how and when the club will require the actual sponsorship cash, giving the sponsor and yourselves some margin. It could well be that your sponsor will require an invoice: this must be properly drawn up as shown in appendix E. Finally, the club should be prepared for all of this to happen as a result of their initial telephone call or letter, and without the formality of any meeting.

APPENDIX D

Why Motorsport ?
- - - - - - - - - -

A carefully formulated motorsport sponsorship plan will meet a large number of promotional and public relations requirements, many of which can be fulfilled by other promotions, but some of which are unique and all of which are fulfilled very cost effectively.

It would be difficult to equal the excitement, colour and glamour that is an inherent part of the motorsporting scene. It can promote your corporate image or advertising message in a modern, dynamic and go-ahead fashion. If speed is an element of your customer service there is no better promotional media.

At the same time the increasing media coverage of motorsport, particularly on TV of recent, is producing a large and growing audience, many of whom will fall within your target audience. It is estimated that over 2,000,000 people actually saw the Lombard RAC Rally in 1981 and in 1983 - 3,000,000. Many people follow the Sunday motor racing on TV , with many attending in person. Blackpool Speed Trials attracts an audience of some 50,000. An average National Rally can fill a town.

A well turned out, smart competition car will always attract the attention of the public and therefore subject it to the sort of scrutiny that can be used to good advantage as an exhibition or show item - inside or out.

It generates interest among your staff and customers, it even promotes its own form of loyalty.

In the case of the motor trade, the sight of a competition car being prepared on your premises or merely on show reflects favourably in the eyes of the customer. "If you're good enough to tune his car, etc, etc".

In short, properly promoted motorsport sponsorship can only benefit the backer by way of exposure, image, an advertising message and in many other ways. It can be refined to fit every need and product.

The Benefit to my Sponsor
- - - - - - - - - - - - - - - -

The opportunity of coverage in the local and national motoring press both at the announcement of the backing and throughout the season.

The opportunity of editorial coverage both in the sponsors and drivers local press throughout the season.

The opportunity of coverage in press releases to the manufacturers P R section, the Club affiliated to the make of car and all Club magazines appertaining to the driver.

The car through its inherent interest and the sponsors livery will make an exciting show piece for publicity. It is also suitable for both inside and outside show static and mobile.

Exposure through competition. Most venues allow the spectators access to the pit and paddock area during the course of an event. Many events attract many thousands of spectators. The car is also seen on the public highway either on a trailer or being driven to and from an event. Today numerous events are televised during peak periods.

As in all promotions the benefit is directly proportional to the effort. The exciting nature of motoring sport makes it an ideal way of entertaining clients. A day out with your car and driver being both a somewhat interesting and memorable occasion.

Motor Sport has a unique promotional property, "T" shirts, stickers, hats and other likewise promotional bric-a-brac are an accepted and expected part of the scene. The ideas are many fold and without end.

Events can be used for displaying your product and/or service. The idea being for the driver to maximise all efforts to benefit your business through effort.

Reproduced by courtesy of Peter Clements Rallying, Middlewich, Cheshire.

01.892.8121

DELTA RACING
164B HEATH ROAD,
TWICKENHAM,
MIDDX.
01-892 8121

Invoice No.
L-MEP 003

Shell Motor Sport Unit,
Shell Lubricants UK,
Cobden House,
Station Road,
Cheadle Hulme,
Cheshire SK8/5AD

23rd January 1985

23rd Jan'y 1985   To sponsorship of Lancia-Martini Endurance
Project 1985 in respect of agreed quantity
of gasoline for record car and supporting
vehicles. Per letter UOMKL/114/CKC/jo 21st
January 1985

800.00

£800.00p

E & O.E.

If we now refer to 'Plan B' of the previous Chapter and assume that 'United Banking' have carefully selected a number of likely back-up sponsors, I would now advise the following strategy:

Supposing 'United' have chosen Shell as a possible supporter of the officials' fuel account, the series co-ordinator should write, or telephone, the appropriate Shell executive giving full details of the championship, together with a brief outline of the publicity on offer. It is quite probable, should Shell be interested, that an agreement could be reached without either a formal meeting or a negotiating discussion. However, should the approach be to a national hotel group with a view to offsetting the large accommodation bill, then 'United's' approach must be in writing; the only exception being in that case where there already exists some sort of relationship between the two parties. Either a personal or written approach will almost certainly result in the hotel group inviting 'United' to discussions should they be interested and in which event it will be to the latter's advantage to produce a mini prospectus. Not as elaborate as the driver's, it should nevertheless outline your history, your budget, the 'named' entries, the publicity on offer, the estimated spectator attendance, media coverage and venue locations. A neatly prepared prospectus, however small, just might impress the group sufficiently to back you, especially if you've also invested in the services of a graphic artist.

Take into consideration the fact that whilst Shell will know exactly what you are talking about, the 'County Hotels' group may not. Despite your letter and subsequent prospectus you may have to tell them all about the sport and its sponsorship merits, mentioning the fact that any deal will include passes for both their clients and staff at each of the eight rounds. Tie up the monetary aspect and especially the dates for settlement. In this respect ask for a contract since their support is intended to cover the entire series of eight rallies. In so doing this will protect both your own interests as well as the sponsor's. In the case of a company like Shell, they will probably insist on a contract and whilst this will protect the candidate's interests, it will also restrict any petroleum advertising to their products only; appendix F.

In conclusion, the candidate should not be surprised to find that any meeting arranged may be brief and almost a formality. This, I can assure you, is more than a probability if you've adhered to the guidelines that I have given.

In this coming section I will deal with the approach and negotiation appertaining to the individual or team who wish to obtain product support. However, before embarking upon this 'excursion' make sure that you really do have something to offer and that any approach cannot be taken, in any way, as scrounging! Castrol, Shell and Silkolene may all be wealthy organisations, but nevertheless they will want value in relation to any help that they might give you. If you have been on a winning streak they will want it to continue, whilst expecting you to promote and publicise their products on every possible occasion. Similarly, they will expect you to keep them informed of your seasonal progress, at the least, month by month. Don't let this put you off. If you possess one national championship, possibly one club series, an occasional independent award and frequent mentions by the media, then you're in with a good chance. A reasonably short letter enclosing a couple of photographs, your plans, a few press cuttings and your record to date might well do the trick. The sort of letter to which I am referring is shown in appendix C, Chapter five along with a specimen reply.

Should you be successful with Castrol for example, you might receive anything from a few litres of oil up to a cash contribution towards your seasonal expenditure. In all probability there will be no formal negotiation and your request will be answered with a straight yes or no! If it is a 'yes' you will be required to sign a contract (see appendix F) and to adhere to certain livery regulations relating to your car. There is really nothing more to obtaining product support than I have described; it is something of a lottery, but mostly it depends on what you have done and what you are going to do.

Whilst product support can be useful, do not overdo the privilege. Even if you are 'God's Gift' to motorsport, don't go mad: four or five such sponsors are quite sufficient for any individual and perhaps eight or nine should you be running a team. Finally, should any reader still not be sure what constitutes this form of sponsorship it is: the supply of accessories, fuel or lubricants free of charge and sometimes cash in return for an agreed amount of promotion and publicity. For example, this support includes such items as anoraks, batteries, brake linings, brake pads, crash helmets, dampers, electrical equipment, fire systems, harnesses, instruments, lights, oil, overalls, petrol, sparking plugs and tyres.

I have left until last the involved business of the approach and negotiation as it applies to the candidate seeking a major sponsorship. I will, therefore, begin by

We have supplied you with two copies of this form. Please complete and sign both and send one in the envelope provided to: **Castrol Sport, PO Box 150, Reading, Berks, RG1 8DF.** Retain the other copy for your reference. As a Castrol Sport contracted driver you will receive the full support of the Castrol organisation, as well as promotional and publicity benefits. To ensure you continue to receive this support all we ask is that you help us in return.

[1]   You must wear the Castrol Sport racewear at and during all race meetings in which you are competing, plus test and press days and other appropriate occasions.

[2]   You must use Castrol lubricants exclusively in your competition vehicle.

[3]   You must advise Castrol immediately following every event of your performance in events via telephone or using the Results Cards provided.

[4]   You should provide Castrol Sport with one black and white quality photograph (suitable for magazine reproduction) of yourself and one of your Castrol Sport liveried vehicle.

[5]   You must notify Castrol Sport of any change of address, vehicle or specification.

[6]   You must carry Castrol Sport livery in the agreed positions on your vehicle.

[7]   The advertising permit is the property of Castrol and if requested you must return it to us. If for any reason the permit is misused we may have to withdraw it. Castrol will look to you to use the licence responsibly and indemnify us for any loss which we might incur by your misuse of the permit, including any loss of Castrol's 'principal permission licence'.

[8]   This agreement applies from the date of signature to December 31st, 1984.

REMEMBER

[1]   You permit Castrol the unrestricted use of your name for advertising purposes or purposes of trade, and of any photograph or picture of you and your vehicle.

[2]   You must not display advertising for any other fuel or oil company, or fuel oil additive manufacturer on your vehicle or self, unless specified to do so as a condition of entry to a particular championship.

Insurance – You must effect adequate insurance with insurers of repute against injury of any nature to third parties and their property arising out of your competition activities. It may be required that you will have to produce to Castrol evidence of such insurance. In any event you will indemnify Castrol against all damages, cost claims and proceedings of any nature whatsoever arising out of your competition activities covered by this document.

I agree to abide by all the conditions above.

Signature ...... *JUNE LAIRD* ...... Date *3. 3. 1984*

Name ......

Address ......

......

assuming that the 'hunter' has selected six suitable companies which seem to fit the bill, so what comes next:

When the sponsorship that is being sought can be described as substantial, the candidate should not approach any prospective sponsor in person unless they are already known to him, or her, or unless an introduction has previously been arranged. If the latter applies then do not hesitate to call or phone, but do so solely as a reminder, concluding the conversation by telling your contact that you will write in a day or two giving them fuller details. Having taken this initiative now you must revert to the procedure which I prescribe for all candidates.

Relying upon the written word, your letter must be sound and trustworthy, and of sufficient length that it will enable you to say all that you want whilst taking into consideration that this communication is only a cover for your prospectus. With regard to your letter, a specimen of which appears on page 49, the general principles to be observed are as follows:

i. Tell the prospect briefly about yourself and your racing achievements.

ii. Tell the prospect why you have selected their company.

iii. Tell the prospect about your future hopes and plans if you were to be sponsored by them.

iv. Do not mention money in your letter, this is in your prospectus.

v. Do not approach your employer. There could be tax or other snags and they may not approve of your leisure activities anyway.

vi. Ensure that you address the package personally to the appropriate recipient as well as indicating that it is 'personal.'

vii. Do not give away your prospectus, even if it is a copy. Ask the prospect to send it back should they be uninterested and, as stated in Chapter five, enclose the necessary stamps for this purpose. This action serves a dual purpose in that it ensures a reply as well as the return of your valuable material.

viii. Try and find a company whose name will blend with that of your car or team.

Although you may find this last item somewhat mute, if you stop and think about it there is good sense in observing this particular rule. If you can find a good blend of names, it is the sort of elementary 'aside' that might just make all the difference to your approach. For example, 'Guyson Pilbeam' and Marlboro' McLaren' do sound much better than, say, 'Benson & Hedges Tyrrell' due to their overall sponsor cum team titles being easier on the tongue than the latter. A good example of this name linking appears in appendix H, 'The Endeavour Brighton Speed Trials;' where Endeavour Garages are the event sponsors.

Before concerning ourselves with the positive or hopeful reply, a word about my specimen approach letters. Some readers might feel that my suggestions spark of both the elementary and the obvious. Whilst seeing the point, I have, however, to say that if I were to accept the premise that we all know what to say, then surely my book would fail in its intention. I'm sure that many of my readers can make a better job of letter writing than I, but I'm forced to say that this isn't always the case. To illustrate what I mean I will permit myself yet another example, the letter that follows was shown to me by a company's PRO during my research for this book. It was dictated by the chairman of one of our bigger motor clubs, who, incidentally, is also a company director;

I quote:
"Dear Sirs,
I represent the 'Blankety Blank' Motor Club. We are seeking a sponsor to help us finance our forthcoming motorsporting season, for which we require £800. Hope you can help us in our quest.

Yours sincerely,
JOHN SMITH (fictitious)
Chairman, BBMC"
Unquote.

ENTRY FORM   **APPENDIX G**   **Complete in block letters**

The <u>Endeavour</u> Brighton National Speed Trials
September 14th, 1985

(National/Restricted Permit Number S/1409/5)

Held under the General Regulations of the RAC Motor Sports Association Ltd. (incorporating the provisions of the International Sporting code of the FIA) and the Supplementary Regulations.

★ A separate Entry Form must be completed for each entry.

This form should be completed in all details and then forwarded, together with the appropriate entry fee, to the Clerk of the Course, Tony Johnstone, c/o Brighton & Hove Motor Club, 22 Braybon Avenue, Brighton BN1 8EA. An incomplete Entry Form may result in refusal of the entry.

ENTRANT

Surname _____   Mr., Mrs., Miss, or Title _____

First Name (for Programme) _____   Other Forenames _____

Address _____

Telephone No. _____
RAC M.S.A. International or National Speed Licence Prefix and No. .... •

DRIVER (if different from above) _____

Surname _____   Mr., Mrs., Miss, or Title _____

First Name (for Programme) _____   Other Forenames _____

Address _____

RAC M.S.A. International or National Speed Licence Prefix and No. .... •

Class ....

Make of Car _____   Model _____

Make of engine _____   c.c. _____

Year of manufacture _____   No. of cylinders _____   Is the car supercharged or turbocharged? _____

If any modifications have been made to the following please give full details:

Compression ratio _____   No. and make of carburettors _____

Valve springs _____   Manifold (Inlet and Exhaust) _____

Cylinder head _____   Bodywork _____

Wheels and Tyres _____

Is your car fitted with a timing strut   YES/NO   (see S.R.'s Para. 16)

Name of Club of which entrant is a member _____

If eligible for Walter Edlin Trophy give B. & H.M.C. Membership No. _____

Warecrete British Sprint Championship Contender   YES/NO   "First ten" Running No. (if applicable) _____

Pubs. 'N Clubs British Sprint Leaders Championship Contender   YES/NO

If any other driver is sharing this car, state name _____

*For entries in Classes 1 or 8 only a Restricted Speed or Clubman's R.S. Licence will suffice.

OFFICE USE ONLY

C of C	S of M		Club H'cap.	No.

P.T.O.

ENTRIES CLOSE ON WEDNESDAY, 14th AUGUST, 1985

★ A Certificate of Speed attained, signed by the Official RAC M.S.A. Timekeeper will be available at £10 if applied for when entering.

QUALIFICATION OF CARS—The onus of ensuring that his car complies with the regulations rests on the Entrant. Competing cars must be maintained in an eligible condition throughout the event. If a car is involved in an accident, the entrant is under the obligation to have the car re-checked by the Scrutineer before continuing the event.

Needless to say the above communication neither brought forth the necessary cash, nor even a reply. I am therefore anticipating that the contents of the above letter will convey to you all why it is sometimes necessary for me to return to the somewhat elementary.

Now I come to the reply that we all hope for: an invitation to visit your prospective sponsor to discuss in detail your recent communication and the proposals therein. First, confirm your acceptance immediately by telephone and later by letter. When phoning this is the time to seek their permission to include any additional person that you may want to take along, not forgetting to name them, their function and relevance in your covering letter. However, on this subject a word of warning: keep this additional invitation to one person only and remember the adage that 'too many cooks spoil the broth'! The sort of person whom you might consider taking along could be your manager or mechanic, whilst a team manager might like to take along one of his drivers, especially if his team includes any big names. Whatever your decision, this person must be instructed to speak only when spoken to or when their expert opinion is directly requested. In other words do not be seen to be 'ganging-up' on your prospect. The sort of invitation you should aim for is shown in appendix G.

Preparing for your 'big day' should be kept simple. Re-check all your data, prepare your answers to routine questions and don't forget to take along your own prospectus as a reminder of what is going to be discussed. More important, however, is the preparation of yourself. Consider seriously that you are probably about to meet a very senior company executive, and that when you do come face to face it will be the first impression that will be the lasting one in his, or her, mind. Do not turn up in jeans, have some regard for his, or her, seniority and respect for his, or her, position. A quick word with your prospect's secretary, before the meeting, might not go amiss if you are in any doubt as to what will be expected of you. You'll find that such an approach could go in your favour, since the aforementioned secretary is bound to relate your query to your prospect in confidence. Having ascertained what you need to know, be prepared when the 'big day' comes to act out the proverb 'When in Rome – do as the Romans do!' Likewise, teach yourself some self-discipline and forget that you are possibly a 'lunatic' in a car and act responsibly whilst in your prospect's presence. Finally, in this context learn all you can about the company and, above all, be prepared to play your entire part by ear.

On the negative side, there is one point which is perhaps worth a mention and that is the 'no reply' situation; an ever increasing hazard of courtesy 1980's style. Going hand in glove with this situation: not only do they not reply, but they also seemingly forget to return your enclosures as well. In such an event allow no more than one week to pass beyond the date when *you think* you should have had a reply, then telephone the recipient's secretary. Request the courtesy of an acknowledgement or the return of your prospectus which was pre-paid. There is always a chance that your prospect has been away or that just such a reminder might prompt the secretary to remind her boss to read his, or her, mail. Such an action has been known to turn up trumps, but there is one rule though: be polite throughout however frustrated you may have become.

Once you do find yourself in the 'hot seat' that is the time to forget yourself and to talk solely about what you aim to do for your prospective sponsor's business. For your part there are three issues upon which you must try to sell your ideas:

i. **Sponsorship as an investment:** Re-affirm that you are there hoping to enter into a purely business arrangement in which there are definite goals at stake. First, you might quote from the Financial

66

APPENDIX H   Advertising · Marketing · Public Relations
Graphic Design & Illustration

ABC Advertising Partners Limited

BMcL/JP

46 Odsal Road · Odsal · Bradford BD6 1AQ
Tel (0274) 306409

11 July 1983

Mrs June Laird

Dear June

Thank you for your letter which has been forwarded on to me by
my client Mr Jim O'Leary, Operations Director, Tordoff Motor Group.
We have discussed the possibility of sponsorship in detail and the
matter has now been left with me to take things a little further.

I would be obliged if we could arrange a meeting to discuss the
contents of your letter and what possible involvement we may have.
Unfortunately, timing is against us as I will be away on holiday
by the time you receive this letter. In the circumstances I
would ask you to be patient until the end of the month, I will
then contact you by 'phone to perhaps arrange a mutually convenient
appointment.

Best wishes.

Yours sincerely

Brian McLindon
MANAGING DIRECOR

Times of October the 23rd, 1980 which stated that sponsorship can attract a great deal of attention at relatively little cost. Second, an involvement in sport can be seen to reflect the company's own competitiveness, whilst the publicity and promotion purchased may be used for a whole year for one single outlay.

ii. Media coverage: First, a reminder should be given to your prospect as to the number of people who follow motorsport, the spectators. Second, the press in an editorial sense. Third, radio and television sports coverage and the cost effectiveness of even the slightest national reference. Fourth, the envy created amongst your rivals through your trade journals referring to the sponsorship and maybe displaying a photograph of your car and its crew.

iii. Taxation advantages: Any outside

A graphic artist might depict a livery such as this to good effect in anyone's negotiating prospectus.

involvement is tax deductable and in fact, as such, sponsorship can be used to form the basis of your customer entertaining for an entire year. However, referring once again to the Financial Times, I quote: 'It should be observed that sponsorship is not a charity. Indeed one sponsor calculates that for an exhibition investment of £15,000, they receive publicity valued at almost ten times that amount. Therefore, when you consider that over half the investment outlay could be offset against corporation tax, the sponsor derived benefit of considerable value partly at public expense.' Unquote. Should you be unable to remember this sort of thing, as a part of your presentation, then by all means refer to notes, since this type of introduction can actually tell your prospect a lot without your actually having to say very much. Follow up by describing how, where and why you decided that they were exactly the company which you sought. For example, I was reading 'Marketing Weekly' and came across your new product. I decided that my

own plans could assist you to develop a market interest by my publicising the product and your company in this context. In any case, you might add, I think that you will agree that an involvement with the 'Andrews Astra' does have that certain something; Andrews being the name of the sponsor concerned and Astra the car.

Having survived the opening banter, next on the agenda will be a detailed discussion of your prospectus and in the main those parts of it which form your plans and your budget. The former data is likely to serve as a preliminary to the more important financial issue and in which respect you must expect to be fairly extensively cross-examined. Do make allowances: your prospect may not know anything about motorsport nor its technicalities, so that your engine rebuilds, test sessions and tyre consumption will all come under scrutiny, whilst the company tries to find some way in which to save money. In such an event, provided that you've done your homework properly, stick by your figures and do not under any circumstances either offer or be cajoled into making cuts; this can spell disaster later on. Let me once again cite a personal experience:

Some time ago I approached an international company for £3,500. At the outset of our negotiations their PRO made it clear that only £2,250 would be available for my purpose. In my eagerness to become associated with them I accepted the reduced offer and as a result of my impetuosity, I spent the next three months worrying about where the deficit would come from knowing that my original budget was correct. Good fortune prevailed and a co-sponsor was found, but never again will I allow this to happen. Therefore, make it a golden rule not to be short changed even if it means declining what is on offer. By and large you are being tested, so remember there are no rewards to be had from an incomplete championship or badly prepared car. It goes

without saying that you'll get very little respect for such an action in the long term, especially if you are the team's captain as I was.

Obviously there are exceptions to this business of short changing and these are:

i. The case where the prospect offers a genuine alternative solution.

ii. The case where the prospect gives you ample time to find a co-sponsor and is agreeable to sharing the publicity gains.

Assuming that you get your budget figure, or whatever, you now have to reach an agreement on how you wish the sponsorship to be paid; lump sum or instalments and when? This latter condition is of the utmost importance and, having been agreed upon, must be confirmed in writing as well as being embodied in the sponsorship contract. Clear this up immediately your negotiations have been concluded ... there is nothing more soul destroying for the candidate than to have his, or her, plans held up on this account. Particularly, it is to your advantage that you know who writes the cheques so that they may also receive a copy of the settlement confirmation and contract. Finally, this person should supply the correct invoice details and the format of same that the sponsor will require; another cause to delay your plans.

With the worst behind you the negotiations will now centre around your publicity return as described in your prospectus yet again. This along with the contractual legality is dealt with in Chapter seven which follows. In concluding this part of your approach it should be noted that you might be required to explain sponsorship fully to your prospect and in particular the technical costs budgeted. Hence the reason why it will pay you to take along an expert to help you to substantiate this; the technical costs usually being the ones totally misunderstood by the lay company. However, it will be the scope of your publicity return that will now be uppermost in your prospect's mind, and which will

Lancia-Martini's record breaking Delta 1.6 exhibits what is meant by multi-sponsorship. The car is seen high on the M.I.R.A. 34 degree banking.

inevitably be the deciding factor in their implementing any provisional agreement reached.

Check list

i. Decide whether or not your initial sponsor approach should be by telephone or in writing. A simple method of resolving such an issue: do you know the prospect? If not, write!

ii. When writing give brief, but concise details of your approach and return. If you are a club or organiser, you might consider producing, and enclosing, a mini-prospectus. However, if you are an individual competitor or team, then you must enclose your prospectus.

iii. Confirm all prospective sponsor's re-

plies in writing; even those who phone.

iv. When you are enclosing a prospectus, ask for its return should the prospect not be interested and do not forget to pre-pay return postage.

v. When choosing a prospective sponsor, try to choose, if at all possible, a firm whose name 'gels' with your own; for example, if your name is McLaren try Marlboro'.

vi. When approaching a product supporter, keep your request within reason.

vii. Once a prospect makes favourable 'noises' keep them informed of anything relevant to your approach.

viii. Should you receive a negotiation invitation, be well prepared. Make sure that you are able to satisfy the prospect as to why motorsport is a good investment. At the same time do not assume that your prospect knows anything about the sport; assume that they don't.

ix. Should you receive such an invitation, prepare yourself. Find out what your prospect will expect you to wear. Learn all you can about the company and finally, this is the time to seek permission should you wish to include anyone else in your invitation; manager, mechanic etc.

x. When attending a sponsorship meeting, do not take the initiative until asked.

xi. When asked how you think that your prospect might benefit, remember the three issues which follow:

Media coverage.

Sponsorship as an investment.

Taxation advantages.

xii. Expect to be cross-examined fairly extensively about the financial aspects of your prospectus. Have your answers and/or experts ready.

xiii. Satisfy yourself whether or not a contract will be necessary, together with its scope. Decide at this stage whether or not you feel that legal representation could be in your interests.

xiv. Should your negotiation prove successful, sort out when and where the sponsorship cash will be made available; this is of the utmost importance. Include this item in any contract or confirmatory document.

xv. Do not, under any circumstances, agree to your needs being reduced unless your prospect has an alternative solution to offer.

Chapter 7

The Publicity Return and Contract

Part A: The publicity return

The sponsor, having heard your 'story', will now want to know what they are going to get in return for the support which they have provisionally agreed to give you. Since this is likely to form the final topic of any discussion, then it will be to your advantage if you spend some time preparing a hand-out which will define this part of any contract, as you see it.

With the exception of the more elementary forms of return which we have already mentioned, the object of this Chapter is to consider, in detail, the advertising and publicity package that will apply to any major sponsorship contract. However, it might be a good idea if I first re-cap on the basic return that is applicable to the more nominal degree of support. Essentially, the smaller sponsor can expect to receive publicity and promotion commensurate with their outlay and its importance to the candidate. For example, if you have entered into an agreement with J.W.E. Banks & Sons to supply you with the 'Koni' shock absorbers, Banks will expect you to display a couple of prominent decals on your car and they will also expect you to keep them regularly informed of your results and media mentions. Finally, they will require the rights to use your name in any of their own advertising and publicity. Therefore, the type of

agreement that would be applicable to 'Koni,' could consist of either a simple letter, as has been my own experience, or an even simpler verbal understanding.

Similarly, the smaller financial sponsor offering cash to a club or organiser, will expect an advertisement in any club literature and at any of the latter's venues. They will expect a mention in all press releases relevant to their support. They will reserve the right to use their beneficiary's name as a part of the company's promotion and publicity programme, whilst any contract, in writing, might again be similar to that of Koni. However, it is probable that it will be somewhat more detailed and elaborate in both its concept and wording.

Negotiating a much larger sponsorship return is, of course, a much more complicated and more technical issue. Therefore, it should come as no surprise to the reader to learn that these negotiations may need to agree as many as fourteen separate aspects of the publicity deal. Hence, it seems to make sense if I describe each in its order of precedence, as follows:

1. Making the best use of any sponsorship deal

It is in the interests of both parties to establish quickly just what each is seeking in return for the sponsorship agreed. It might be argued that a sponsor investing a few thousand pounds must obviously be

72

seeking a fairly substantial return; it should follow, but it doesn't! The candidate might have a reason for wanting the publicity to go one way, the sponsor another. Therefore, it is essential that early in the proceedings such a matter must be resolved, so that both sides will feel that the best use is going to be made of the investment.

2. Level of benefit

Obviously anyone taking part in a sponsored sport should seek the maximum publicity both for their sponsor and for themselves, but what has to be agreed upon is the right balance. The sponsor cannot benefit if the participant 'hogs' the limelight, nor can the latter benefit if the situation is reversed. Similarly, there may be two major sponsors sharing the participant, in which case it is even more important to strike a balance between all the parties at the outset. Get it straight just how widespread each one of you wants your own part of the publicity to go: a matter that will require much discussion, but which should not be left to chance. In this respect the candidate should organise his, her or their own publicity programme to coincide with that of the sponsor, thus avoiding the 'hogging' syndrome.

3. Media coverage

Of vital importance to these discussions will be the spread of the sponsorship's media coverage in magazines, in newspapers, on radio, through spectators and on television. When talking about this issue it is prudent to assume that your sponsor does not know who your media outlets are, nor you theirs. Therefore, make sure that this subject is brought into the open, and that someone is appointed to act as press officer; preferably not you, the candidate. Lastly don't forget to highlight the journalistic adage that 'one inch of editorial is worth a full page of advertising.'

4. Displays and exhibitions

One possible use that a sponsor might make of a competitor and his, or her, car is their attendance at company displays and exhibitions. Both have the same motive: the creation of prestige in the eyes of the sponsor's clients and competitors, whilst likewise, creating a spirit of one-upmanship amongst their staff. There are however, two snags: first, ensure before you get involved, in any form of active promotion, that such an idea will not interfere with your events or test sessions. Second, should you be contracted to drive someone else's car make sure that it is going to be available for the dates in question and confirm any arrangement in writing, adding, in your own interests, a penalty clause incumbent upon both your sponsor and the car's owner. Should this surety seem somewhat drastic, take yet another leaf out of my book of experience. I was recently let down by a large Italian car concessionaire, who, having agreed to make a particular car available for such an exhibition, then proceeded to provide a 'look alike,' which wasn't! In this instance my arrangements had been minuted, since they also affected a number of colleagues and so therefore, despite some minor embarassment this got me off the hook with my sponsors. In short, don't trust anyone; not even those who claim to have a 'name.'

5. Incentive schemes

Motorsport involvement can be used for company promotion in a multitude of ways, some of which are incentive schemes like those which follow:

i. Catalogues

Entice your clients and potential clients to accept your brochure by using the car and its driver as a cover feature.

ii. Exhibitions

Whilst already mentioned, another reason for displaying a race or rally car has to be to attract attention. Involvement in any form of exhibition can be expensive, so that this can be seen as being one way of stopping the business visitor in their tracks. The exhibit can also be used as a useful conversation piece that will lead to your inviting the onlookers to take a closer look at the car and, inevitably, your own products.

iii. Incentive gifts
Offer your sales staff bonus prizes that can be linked to your racing or rallying involvement. Start off in a minor way by offering them a few complimentary tickets, working towards the time when you might offer your more successful salesmen a drive in the competitor's car in return for a specified turnover increase.

iv. Promotional investment
A tastefully liveried car and its transporter vehicle can be used as a means of launching new projects, as well as an added means of upgrading the company's existing image.

v. Publicity incentive
Create competitions amongst your customers; giving them the use of the car and its crew as first prize. Similarly, you can also create an incentive for your customers to attend your marketing conferences by inviting your driver to give a short talk ... with the car.

vi. Public awareness
Increase your corporate image by bringing your company to the consumer through the aid of shopping precinct displays and other direct attractions.

Any one of the foregoing may be seen as creating an incentive to invest in motorsport over and above any other sport. After all it is only logical to assume that a dartboard or snooker cue will hardly command the same attention that must surround any form of motorsporting machinery.

6. Entertaining.
An increasing number of companies are finding that the opportunity presented by entertaining guests at a sporting event can be essential to their overall marketing strategy. The aim being to give important customers and suppliers, a day to remember, and one which they will associate with your company long after. Motorsport is ideal for just such a purpose: it is exciting, fast, glamorous and more than any other leisure activity has a special magic all its own. Properly used, this is an especially potent force not to be treated as merely 'a day at the races!' To help you to ensure that such a day out is even more memorable, most of the leading race venues are able to offer hospitality suites within which your guests can avail themselves of a first class meal, whilst enjoying a more or less unrestricted view of the racing and trackside activities. These facilities are readily available at competitive rates, Silverstone, for example, having over fifty suites giving panoramic views all round. Likewise, the more important rallies usually have on hand similar units, but of the more mobile variety. Finally, most static suites are accessible to the pit and paddock areas, so that your guests can indulge in the many fascinating things which go on behind the scenes.

Obviously the selection of your guests for this purpose will require careful consideration and a modicum of discretion, but might be categorised thus:

i. Important existing customers
This can be a memorable reward for past and present business transacted.

ii. Important potential customers
How better to sell your company's wares than away from *that telephone* which continuously interrupts your very important negotiations.

iii. Customers' families
Such a day out will help the family to feel a part of your customers' work. Likewise, a team 'Tee' shirt will serve as a longstanding reminder to the children of a superb, but different, day to remember.

iv. Journalists
An invitation to the more important of these might give your company an improved image in next month's trade paper.

v. Staff
An invitation to a lucky few will have them

talking about their employer long after office hours, and more especially in the pub amongst their colleagues and friends.

7. Linking the name
The media refers to an attempt to obtain free publicity by name dropping as being 'Blatant Advertising!' This attitude has unfortunately rung the death knell on many a sound sponsorship at birth; it can be accepted as being one of the participant's and sponsor's prime predicaments. In the main the trouble concerns the naming of the sponsor in the press, on the radio and on TV. You can tell the latter's editorial staff that your club, your team or yourself are being sponsored by 'Bloggs Crisps,' but trying to get 'Bloggs' a mention is another story. Your Mr. Average sports or features editor will have been warned a thousand times not to upset their advertising manager. Therefore, try as you might, it is almost a certainty that your sponsor will be ignored unless they already have a hefty advertising account with that particular medium. No matter how strongly you voice your protestations, nothing will be resolved without your convincing your already over-extended sponsor to spend more money advertising in the offending publication or whatever. They probably won't agree and what is worse is that it will be you that will get the blame for the media's omission. Fortunately there is a way of defying our NUJ friends, it is called 'linking the name' and has already been loosely mentioned in Chapter six.

If McLaren were to announce that Alain Prost had won last week's 'Utopian' Grand Prix in their Marlboro' backed car or if the BARC, likewise, announced that their 'Wendy Wools' championship had been won by 'Jack Frost,' then you can bet your life that, other than the motoring press, most of the popular media will 'conveniently' forget to name 'Marlboro' or 'Wendy Wools'. What you have to do is this: call the car a 'Marlboro' 'McLaren' and the contest the 'Wendy Wools BARC Special Saloon Car Championship,' you then draw up a document registering this fact or, better still, do it legally through your solicitors. Should your full name still not be mentioned by the media, you will then be entitled, legally, to both an apology and a correction in the next edition, or in the next programme or whatever. It might be devious, but for a comparatively small sum it will protect your mutual interests. Of course there will always be the 'Clever Dick' who will mention only the driver and nothing else. In this event clarify the title chosen with a statement linking the driver's name as well, whilst similarly, it is also a good idea, when the time comes for any press releases, for you to make it clear that your titles are a registered combination. Only then will you feel free from this 'blatant advertising' syndrome.

8. Press embargo
Sometimes it is prudent to keep the details of one's sponsorship a secret. You may not want the opposition to know what you are about, whilst alternatively, your sponsor might want to announce your liaison at a time best suited to their plans. Inevitably there will always be the odd leakage or rumour, both of which can be alleviated by yourself or your sponsor declaring a press embargo. This can be implemented by the forwardance of a declaration to this effect to those elements of the media most likely to be concerned. However, most candidates will recognise that the need to employ such a measure will only apply to the better known company or participant.

9. Pre-event publicity
The opposite of the foregoing item 8. Part of the overall returns strategy might be to distribute, via a press conference or similar get-together, a mountain of releases aimed at announcing your union and your sponsor's plans. Such a press release might either be dictated at the meeting or handed out in brochure form, and will embody all the relevant information, together with any publicity illustrations and photographs.

10. Promoting the participant

This is something for the candidate's own conscience. If you imagine yourself to be motorsport's answer to Henry Cooper or Felicity Kendall, then you could suggest that you appear in your sponsor's television and other commercials. This could give both parties a sense of being involved in each other's business. However, before you come out with such an idea make sure that your attributes can, in some way, be related to your sponsor's world of breakfast cereals or fitted kitchens. Likewise, also ensure that you really might be a far better prospect for the part than Henry or Felicity!

11. The collation of press mentions

This is normally the sponsor's responsibility and in the case of most multi-national companies a press agency is retained for this purpose; their job being to extract all mentions relevant to their employers from any source. On the other side of the coin,

The best of two worlds: Guyson Euroblast Chief, Jim Thomson, not only advertises on his own car, but also lends support to the B.A.R.C.'s Yorkshire Centre ... see background.

Circuit sponsorship – Oulton Park. ➤

most smaller firms will know their press outlets, thus enabling them to entrust the job of collation to an office junior.

12. Collating those press mentions emanating from such private sources as club bulletins and other similar literature

In contrast to item 11, the question of who collates those mentions referred to above will rest fairly and squarely upon the candidate. In this respect it is your business to keep your sponsor informed about anything, from your end, which mentions their name, their product or their service.

13. Delegating the publicity workload

Another important question is who is going to ensure that the publicity is put to the best use, and who it is that will, similarly, make the best use of any promotional opportunity that may arise. All too frequently a sponsor will attempt to manipulate the participant into accepting this duty, saying that they haven't the staff to spare or to whom such a job can be entrusted. If this happens make it clear that your time is limited and that you already have your own side of the sponsorship to look after. Taking such an action will require diplomacy, but you can temper your rebuff by suggesting that they contact a public relations or publicity agency to look after this for them even if it is going to cost a little extra. Again, if you're into PR as a means of full-time employment you must accept that in this particular context you are a competition driver and nothing more. In practice the candidate will find that it is the smaller sponsors that are the ones likely to try and pass the buck in this way, in the main most multi-nationals are already set up for the purpose of promotion and publicity.

14. Decals and signwriting

Although a relatively minor point, the cost of producing self-adhesive decals or for signwriting your car is one which can easily cause you financial strain. Reverting yet again to my own experience, I was once sponsored solely to compete in four Prescott speed hillclimbs. However, since I was at the same time also sponsored separately for other events, I was faced with having to re-decal my car for the Prescott sponsor over the top of those which already existed. This state of affairs necessitated the production of sixteen decals to cover the four rounds, using four signs per event and too late I realised that I had failed to finalise their payment. In

consequence I added the £72 for this purpose to my sponsorship invoice and the balloon went up. Naturally my sponsor paid, but needless to say I didn't get their support again for the following season!

Tie up not only who pays for the decals or signwriting, but also who pays for the eventual removal of the signwriting which could involve a complete respray. The contention among competitors is that this should be the sponsor's responsibility, but it does need clarification, since it can be very costly and something likely to cause you acute embarassment. Likewise agree upon the parts of your car or transporter vehicle that your sponsor has bought in terms of advertising and the livery that they will require, whilst not forgetting to consider any space you have earmarked for other sponsors and especially that of your trade supporters. It is too late to amend an intricately signed car once it's been painted. Finally, agree who is going to pay for the RAC advertising permit and the more important Entrant's licence, the contention also being that this should again fall to the sponsor.

Summarising part 'A' of this Chapter, there are as you have read, many ways in which motorsport involvement can benefit a company through sponsorship. These can be condensed as being the initiation of a beneficial liaison in which the driver or team will assist your company to achieve its immediate marketing aims through advertising, exposure, image building, promotion, publicity and salesmanship. In the main however, it is essential that all candidates give priority to their own position. In this context you will either be a driver or a team manager, but what you're unlikely to be is a publicity expert. Therefore, do not give in to being used as one, no matter who your sponsor is. In conclusion take into account the impression that a well devised sponsorship can create both within and without motorsport. Anything that is favourable is talked about long after the event and, in this case, it is usually the sponsor's name or product that is recalled long before your name or your car's. Of course this is the whole object of the sponsorship scene as we are all very much aware and which the candidate should not forget.

Part B: The contract

The drawing up of a contract in any guise obviously forms the most important phase of any negotiation or transaction. In its mildest form a contract can be a simple written agreement, whilst in its most complex, one could possibly argue that it is essential to fair play on both sides and therefore must be legally binding. Unfortunately, there is no hard and fast rule as to the layout and content of such a document due to every arrangement being subject to differing clauses. Hence, each and every case must be contracted on its own merits.

When dealing with the subject of financial backing, the complexity of such a contract cannot be seen as being statutory. It might well be that a particular arrangement can be dealt with in the more simple terms of a letter, whilst in another the sponsor or participant may insist upon a properly drawn up legal document. Obviously, it all depends on the degree of support being negotiated, but it can likewise depend on many aspects which either party see as possibly affecting their relationship both favourably and vice versa. In addition, the on-going basis of any deal must also be taken into account, so that there can be no definite ruling as to what should be included or even when a legal contract is necessary.

Shown at appendix 'J' is a letter which formed a type of contract that existed between myself and a sponsor in the sum of £500. A quick glance through this agreement reveals not only its simplicity, but also a number of omissions. This latter state of affairs will come as no surprise to my readers when confronted with the fact that all the sponsorship discussions were

KNIBBS (Manchester) Ltd

Registered number 274836 England

Midland Street Garage
off Ashton Old Road, Manchester M12 6LB
(Registered office)

061-273 4411 (10 lines)

BMS/jhn

Mrs. J. Laird,
289, Norris Road,
Sale,
Cheshire.

17th March, 1983.

Dear Mr. and Mrs. Laird,

I acknowledge receipt of your letters and confirm our telephone conversations over the past two weeks.

Firstly I would like to sincerely apologise on behalf of Lancia, Heron and ourselves on the manner in which your request for sponsorship has been handled. Unfortunately, as you are now aware discussions were taking place with regard to the future of the franchise, and this uncertainty made it extremely difficult to give you any decision.

Perhaps in hindsight it would have been advisable at the outset to say that it was not our policy to support sponsorship and whilst I accept that this would have been unpalatable to you, it would have enabled you to pursue other avenues.

However, it does seem that Lancia personnel at both local and national level, and perhaps even Heron personnel gave you grounds for optimism which were clearly unfounded.

Let us now hope that the enclosed cheque for £500 can be used to our mutual benefit. Your acceptance of this cheque implies of course that:-

1) You will display on your car as prominently as possible the 'Knibbs' logo stickers which will be supplied.
2) You will similarly display Lancia stickers.
') You will use your best endeavours to obtain as much publicity as possible for both Lancia and Knibbs from your participation in events.
4) You will keep us informed of your progress so that additionally we also can extract publicity as appropriate.
5) You will make the car available to us for short term display and be prepared to be present at Showroom and allied type promotional activities should we so desire.

It is of course understood that if there is any clash of dates your active participation in an event would take precedence.
6) That you will use your best endeavours at all times to promote both our company and the Lancia manufacturer and that you will not do anything which would be prejudicial to us.

I look forward to a good relationship between us and wish you every success in the coming season.

Yours sincerely,
for Knibbs (Manchester) Limited,

B. M. Singleton
Managing Director.

DIRECTORS: C. WARBRICK, T.ENG. (C.E.I.), M.I.M.I. (CHAIRMAN)
B.M. SINGLETON, F.C.I.S., F.I.A.C. (MANAGING) G. GADSBY, (SEC),
R.H. HARGREAVES, T.D.LL.B., I.L. BLACK.

A BURNS ANDERSON COMPANY

conducted through a third party. For example, once again there has been no account taken of the decalling costs, whilst it seems, the sponsor was also hoping that I would see to everything. Both these points were rectified in a later telephone call and in this case Messrs. Knibbs passed the promotion and publicity package to their somewhat reluctant advertising agent. The lesson here, being that I should have insisted on an eyeball to eyeball negotiation with the right person from the outset.

Essentially, if the financial arrangement is of either a complex or reasonably substantial nature, then draw up a legal contract and if necessary involve the sponsor's legal advisers in its constitution. In any event the important issues, as far as both parties are concerned, are those which might require to be included in any contract as follows:

i. The sum agreed.

ii. The method of payment to the participant(s).

iii. The extent of the publicity package and who is going to be responsible for its administration.

iv. The rights of the sponsor.

v. The rights of the participant(s).

vi. The sponsors livery requirements.

vii. An agreement as to who will pay for the decalling or signwriting and any subsequent removal of the latter.

viii. An agreement as to who will pay for the RAC advertising permit and Entrants licence.

ix. Safeguarding the security of your sponsorship from other participants (see Chapter nine).

x. Failure to fulfill contract, both parties.

xi. Action to be taken in the event of any 'force majeure.' This clause is one that I feel requires a brief explanation: 'Force majeure' can be loosely described as any major circumstance – good or bad – which is more than likely totally unforeseen. An example being the accident which writes off the car and – sadly – in some cases also the driver. It has been my experience that most sponsors will readily agree to the inclusion of a clause that will absolve the participant from any action which might be taken by them to claim monies already invested.

xii. An agreement relating to co-sponsors and/or product sponsors.

The foregoing items should be easily interpretable without any prolonged explanation. However, item 'ix' may raise a few eyebrows, but it is a very necessary contingency as will be fully explained in Chapter nine. In concluding this final part of the sponsorship negotiation, a word of warning; beware of entering into any sponsorship deal in which the sponsor declines to enter into a legal or written agreement. Many a participant has been 'left on the line' due to an incompleted or uncontracted arrangement.

Finally, the appendices to this Chapter include a number of relevant items which will help to illustrate a few of the points I have made.

Check List

i. Establish exactly what you and your sponsor want by way of a publicity return.

ii. Establish a balance between you, as to just how much each party is going to figure in the promotion and publicity aspect of the liaison. Do not attempt to 'hog' the limelight.

iii. Agree the extent of the sponsorship's media involvement. Do not overlook the advantage of editorial mentions.

iv. When agreeing to attend displays or exhibitions, don't forget the snags and tie up any arrangement watertight.

v. Suggest the use of 'incentive schemes' as a part of the sponsorships promotional and publicity return; see text.

vi. Establish how best both parties can involve the public.

vii. Establish how your sponsor views the publicity aspect of sponsorship and suggest at least five relevant ideas; see text.

M&R-MARTINI & ROSSI LIMITED 80 HAYMARKET LONDON SW1Y 4TG (REGISTERED OFFICE)
REGISTERED NUMBER 305960 ENGLAND

MARTINI & ROSSI

MARTINI & ROSSI LIMITED·NEW ZEALAND HOUSE 80 HAYMARKET LONDON SW1Y 4TG
TELEPHONE: 01 930 3543 TELEX: MARLON G 8813548

6th March 1985

Dear June

After an embarrassingly long delay, due to my almost total absence
from the office following Nuneaton, I am at last writing to thank
you personally for your enormous contribution to the success of
the Lancia Martini Endurance Project.

Heartiest congratulations to you from both Lancia and all of us here
are very much the order of the day. Not simply because you conceived
the record breaking idea originally, nor because you then proceeded
to be very substantially involved with preparation for the event,
but primarily because as Captain you performed magnificently
throughout, leading the team in exemplary fashion from the front and
putting on brilliantly disciplined high speed drives just when they
were most needed.

Under your very positive leadership morale amongst the team remained
high at all times and, despite appalling weather conditions, well
deserved success eventually belonged to you all. Well done indeed.

I have of course also written to Les Girls and, for the sake of good
order, a copy letter is enclosed. It goes without saying, I hope,
that whatever is written to them applies equally to you but
understandably I did want to enlarge in respect of your own very
personal and positive contribution.

I do hope you will keep in touch and that we shall meet again in the
not too distant future. Meantime, drive carefully (what a cheek!)
and have a wonderfully successful '85 season.

Kindest regards,

Yours sincerely

Antony I.H. Beardmore
Group Public Relations Consultant

"MARTINI" AND "M&R" ARE REGISTERED TRADE MARKS

viii. Of the utmost importance is the linking of your sponsors name to that of your car, club, organisation or team. This must be fully covered by some form of agreement, legal or otherwise. However, don't forget your own individual name when finalising this point.

ix. Decide how early you wish the liaison to be publicised. Especially, you should keep a 'beady' eye on the opposition!

x. Discuss how a public announcement can best be made; press conference or what?

xi. Decide upon your own promotion and publicity; this must be thoroughly discussed with your sponsor. It is always an idea to suggest that they might include you in their overall advertising policy.

xii. Establish that your sponsor will be responsible for the collation of all press mentions relevant to themselves. In this respect remember that you are a participant and not a publicity agent.

xiii. You can however, agree to your collating all club and other private mentions.

xiv. Do not become involved in the overall publicity workload, but agree who will.

xv. Finally, and most important: sort out the whole matter of who is going to pay for the necessary decals and/or signwriting. Likewise, agree the space to be provided, as well as who is going to pay for their removal where applicable.

Part B: The Contract

i. Insist on, at least, a written agreement for any nominal sponsorship, and a proper contract once the amount agreed exceeds a £1,000.

ii. Refer to the twelve clauses in the text when drawing up such a document.

iii. If your sponsorship is substantial, you should, in your own interests, consult a solicitor.

iv. Beware of the sponsor who suggests a 'gentleman's agreement', unless it is for a very small sum.

Pre - Event Press Release

LANCIA MARTINI LADIES TEAM

SET TO BREAK ENDURANCE RECORDS

Lancia and Martini are again joining forces on the track. This time with a team of four British lady drivers in an attempt to break eighteen national speed and endurance records.

Using a production Lancia Delta HF Turbo, with its 1600 twin-cam engine, the Lancia Martini ladies team will be going for its record breaking run after some two hours practice on the MIRA track. All of the four team members have considerable motor sport experience at local and national level though they all admit that this speed/endurance run will be a once in a lifetime challenge, particularly as all of the current records are held by men.

Starting at 3 p.m. and running through the night, the record attempt will be scrutinised by the RAC at MIRA's (Motor Industry Research Association) oval test track over the weekend 23rd/24th February. It is the long distance/ endurance records which the team will be particularly keen to break. The 24 hour record of 77.31 m.p.h. was taken by Tony Dron, Andy Rouse and Win Percy driving a Porsche 924 at Snetterton in 1979.

The 2,000 Kilometre record was also taken by a 924 Porsche at Snetterton in 1979. This time the team comprised Gerry Marshall, Tony Lanfranchi, Roger Pierpoint and Chris Nicholson.

Lancia and Martini are closely linked in both rallying and endurance racing at international level through the works Lancia-Martini team operating out of Turin.

This current project is being organised by Lancar Limited, the U.K. concessionaires for Lancia in conjunction with Martini and Rossi Limited in Great Britain.

For further information contact:
Lancia: Paul Ormond
Martini: Tony Beardmore

Chapter 8

Advertising and Sponsorship Agencies

When one examines a subject as complex as sponsorship, amongst the many factors which will both act in a candidate's favour and vice versa will be the agencies that you are likely to come across along the way. These are the advertising agent, who is akin to the sponsor and the publicity-cum-sponsorship agent, who is akin to the candidate. Whilst I have to admit that they both have their uses, I'm sure that many will subscribe to the fact that, similarly, they both have their failings as well.

If I examine the advertising agent first, we must all appreciate that such agencies can equally go hand in glove with firms of all sizes and that they are not necessarily solely retained by the larger multi-national and international groups. From my own experience these agents fall into three categories: those that are anti-motorsport, those that are pro-motorsport and those that remain non-committal. In this respect I will describe each in turn.

Advertising agents who are anti-motorsport

If you are unfortunate enough to come across this category then you will have problems. As is the way of fate, this one usually comes hand in glove with the genuinely interested sponsor prospect that you've taken so long to find. To start with,

the agent won't like motorsport as a publicity medium, anymore than they will like Darts or any other type of sporting activity for that matter. They will prefer the big money that can be earned from television commercials and will go to great lengths to try and persuade your prospect that no one can read anything flashing past at 150mph. Once you've successfully parried this observation by pointing out that they should try watching TV in addition to selling it, they will set about trying to ensure that their client gets the prime pick of the car, the overalls, the service vehicle and so on. They will attempt to re-write the RAC's advertising rules to suit themselves and their client, they will deliberately produce oversize decals and stencils commenting that the RAC/MSA size is far too small. Finally, they will continuously interfere with the publicity return by over-stating that they are the experts and that you are not, whilst upsetting the event organisers by turning up with double the entourage for which the participant is entitled to complimentary tickets. In short, these agents don't want to become involved in motorsport and so should be avoided. Find out if your prospect retains such an agent and, if so, what their attitude is towards your sport and sponsorship? Fortunately they do not all act in the way that I have described, but many do. Should you eventually succeed in 'calling the tune' with them, you can rest assured that you won't get the chance next year!

Advertising agents who are pro-motorsport

This agent is more often than not associated with the indecisive prospect. Diametrically opposite to the previous category, you can thank your lucky stars if you land one of these. They will not only convince your prospect that your proposal is worthwhile, but they will likewise take most of the sponsorship's promotional package under their expert wing. There is however, one snag and that is that your would-be sponsor will be unlikely to tell you that their agent is all for you. If you find the prospect deliberately evading questions about the existence of such an agency, then you can bet your life that this will be the one on your side. Find out if one exists and who they are by resorting to whatever means you can. Time spent sifting out this information will not go amiss, even if your hunch is wrong.

The advertising agent who is non-committal

This category comes in two guises: first, those that are not sure because they honestly don't understand the sport or its ramifications. Second, those that appear to be acting dumb. The former reaction is perfectly natural and will probably be divulged by the sponsor prospect. In this instance don't be afraid to inform ... they will appreciate any additional information that will enhance their existing expertise. You could quite easily strike up something of a rapport with this category, and it is not beyond the bounds of possibility that you might actually become their sports consultant in the future. The second guise you will spot right away. They will pretend to be unsure or indecisive, hoping that you'll go away. These agents l ave two objects in mind: first, to convince your prospect that he doesn't know what he is getting involved in and second, to use their pretence at ignorance to ensure that it will be their client together with themselves who will gain from the liaison, whilst you will be left out in the cold.

By and large any dealing which incorporates an advertising agent should be approached with the utmost caution. In the main these organisations make their living from the high technology world of television commercials, glossy monthlys, promotional literature and public relations in general. Very few seem to take kindly to their clients investing in motorsport, so that those agents who do appear supportive need careful screening as to both their intentions and motives. This situation is probably one of the many reasons that surround the seemingly reluctant attitude of British firms towards the whole spectrum of sponsorship. However, there are those agents who can be relied upon and who, once found, can be a Godsend. Ending on a more cheeful note, I must say that those firms who employ their own advertising and publicity staff are still the best ones to go for, as opposed to those that retain an advertising agent.

A cursory glance through the classified advertisements of most popular motorsporting journals will reveal those agents who constitute the publicity-cum-sponsorship specialists who claim to be able to do everything from merely preparing your prospectus to managing your entire show. In most cases they do a good job and can be a boon to the participant, but there is however, a very big proviso: offering a service designed to take the drudgery out of your motorsporting activities, they will claim to be able to do most things from merely administering your entries to eventually finding you a sponsor and these claims can only be substantiated if the participant is prepared to pay. Generally most of the services they offer are conscientiously executed, my only

Whilst unusual, the logo on John Meredith's Clan Crusader might be a trifle difficult to read at speed.

reservation to this being their claim that they can find you a sponsor. In this respect I am sure that it will come as something of a surprise that my doubts do not revolve around the agencies, but solely around the candidates who seek their assistance in this way. Anyone reading this book must, by now, readily admit that the business of finding a sponsor is one which demands a great deal of time and effort. It is within these two latter facts that the problems appear to lie, a fact confirmed by the principals of two such agencies.

First of all it appears that most candidates of whatever status who approach such an agency commence the relationship by seeking guarantees. How on earth can any agent proffer such a surety? It is the equivalent of a firm that engages an advertising agent to prepare a television commercial, expecting the said agent to guarantee the cost effectiveness of the advert. What it really amounts to is a

reluctance on the part of the participant to spend money. One agent told me of one client who promised payment in advance, as per the agency's terms, and who persuaded the agent to commence his work on the basis of this promise. Eventually after a number of long distance calls from the agent, the client announced that he would only pay once the sponsor had been found. This was not the deal, nor the 'Gentleman's Agreement.' On being informed of possible litigation, the guilty party then set about trying to 'black' the agency. Likewise, another quoted a case that involved the 'head' of a well known racing team: this person was accompanied by one of the aforesaid agent's staff to an important negotiation over 200 miles away from base. After the meeting the racing entrepreneur politely, but firmly declined to pay the agency's fees and expenses due to the mission's failure! Need I say more.

This sort of behaviour is of course not on. If an agent sets about doing his job he, or she, is entitled to be paid and, what is more in advance. The preparation, the research and search can all be costly in terms of hotel expenses, petrol, phone calls, postage, prospectus production and travelling expenses. Most publicity and sponsorship agencies do a worthwhile job given time and money, but it is both impossible and unreasonable to expect from them either a guarantee or a miracle. Normally their fees commence at £30 for a consultation, rising to something around £200 for producing your prospectus and upwards of £500 plus expenses to go sponsor searching. A positive result might set you back a £1,000 or so, but can be considered money well spent if you finally get the sponsorship you seek. It could even cost you more if the sum that you seek is anything really substantial. The choice of using a sponsorship agency is, of course, that of the candidate, but having engaged one for goodness sake don't expect them

As opposed to the previous example clarity is exemplified in this Oulton Park shot of Vince O'Mahoney's 530i BMW.

to work for nothing. Similarly, it doesn't make any difference whether such an agent works from a flashy office or merely from home; both can be equally effective ... if you pay.

The agents I interviewed cited rally crews, particularly, as being amongst their biggest cashflow problems. In this respect do not misunderstand this statement, I have solely repeated the experiences and observations of several agents. However, having once been a rally driver myself perhaps a few observations of my own may not go amiss:

First, it would appear that, cost-wise, rallying has gone through the roof. Part of the blame for this resting fairly and squarely on that good old British institution, the Forestry Commission and their appalling fees. Second, the abundance of equipment and people that now appear to be necessary, even for the most novice team. Third, the sport itself has always had a reputation for attracting the novice

competitor in the mistaken premise that it is safer than circuit racing; a fantasy usually put to good use when confronting a worrying parent. The fact remains that it is expensive even at the most junior level, so that many participants who approach one of the sponsorship agents described are looking for an instant miracle and, worse still, an undertaking **for free** that the said agent will come up with the 'goodies'. Some I am told, even resort to including an agent's fees in their budget under different guises so that the unsuspecting sponsor will pay. Since most of the adverse comments that I heard were directed at this branch of our sport and particularly its novices, perhaps this might be an opportune place for me to offer these competitors some sound advice.

Sport may be likened to a drinking glass in that you only get out what you put in. Therefore, however much you may want to compete make sure that you can afford to do so before you start. In those cases where money is tight, it might be best to mature your skills by taking part in lesser events which will enable you to build up the required track record that should attract sponsorship. Such an action might also enable you to build up the confidence of your bank manager without whom nought will be possible anyway. Remember then that like the 'drinking glass' any publicity agent will insist, quite rightly, that you must put something in before you start.

In bringing this Chapter to a conclusion, I must say that there are competitors in the other branches of motorsport who are also guilty of failing to pay their dues. In almost every agency that I researched I was satisfied that the work for which they were contracted had been carried out exactly provided that they had been given time and paid their fees. If retained in conjunction with some of your own efforts, then you should find them agreeable to giving you some sort of discount thus substantiating their own bona fides. In any event they are all worthy of consideration, even if only in the most basic terms of expert advice at a relatively low cost.

Chapter 9

Rules of the 'Game'

The basic concept of this book is, as its title suggests, both fundamental and self descriptive, 'How to Get Sponsorship for Motorsport.' However, as my readers will have ascertained there is much more to it than the title may suggest and moreover it can be a most complex subject requiring not only a carefully considered plan, but also a modicum of marketing sense. Having taken you carefully through the various steps leading up to the successful negotiation of a sponsorship, now I must clarify the numerous things which you must or must not do, together with any pitfalls that you are likely to encounter along the way. Simplicity being paramount, first I will define the few elementary items that make up those things that you must do if your quest for sponsorship is to succeed.

Part A: Positive rules

i. Always confirm everything in writing.

ii. Keep your word regarding your intention and insist upon the same standard from your sponsor.

iii. Keep your prospective sponsors' names confidential until your sponsorship with one or another is finalised.

iv. Make sure that you attempt at all times to give your sponsor(s) the exposure they expect and which was agreed under the terms of your own publicity responsibility.

v. Keep your sponsor(s) informed of all that you are doing, whether it be a success or otherwise.

vi. Let your sponsor know as soon as possible should you have any programme alterations or cases of 'force majeure'.

vii. When competing remember whom you are representing and, at least, try to finish in one piece.

viii. Tie up every aspect of the sponsorship with a contract or written agreement.

ix. Keep copies of all relevant correspondence incoming and outgoing, whilst ensuring that everything of importance is typewritten.

x. Keep all accounts relevant to the sponsorship deal; even when settled.

xi. Keep copies of all published press material.

xii. Be sure that the signwriting or decals on your car are legible at high speed and watch out for those designs and colours that might lack clarity.

xiii. Lastly, remember that your sponsor comes first.

Part B: Negative rules

i. Approach your sponsor prospect at the

very most two-handed. If you're considering taking along your entire team ... forget it, your prospect will see it as a 'gang-up.'

ii. During the initial stages of any negotiation do not take the initiative, always allow your prospect to put their points of view first.

iii. Consider the effect of a rehearsed approach, this could kill off your chances at the outset. Play it by ear and do not attempt to play act your interview.

iv. Give yourself or your team a name that means something and embody this in your headed notepaper. Do not write anything important freehand or on a plain notepad, you might be mistaken for a novice, whilst any approach using the latter is likely to be terminated via the waste bin. A neat letterhead describing yourself as 'John Smith Racing' could do you a power of good, as well as arousing the recipient's curiosity.

v. If your prospect is a multi-national company, or bigger, do not call in person in the first instance. Unless you have an 'IN', always write giving a brief CV and enclosing your prospectus.

vi. Do not approach your employer. You are putting them 'on the spot.' First, any help could affect your tax. Second, you may well be drawing attention to yourself with the company's pension fund or superannuation insurers who, as sure as God made little green apples, will liken you to the office hang-glider pilot ... as good as dead!

vii. Do not go back for more, this is taboo! You might be lucky once, but its an evens bet that your sponsor won't be impressed. Therefore, do not underestimate your sponsorship requirement; not only will you suffer a loss of face, but more than likely the loss of your sponsor as well.

viii. Do not go back a second time to a prospect who has already declined your proposals, this never works. If the company were unsure the first time, they will be even more so the second.

ix. Do not promise anything that you may not be able to substantiate, this makes far more enemies than friends.

x. Do not rely upon anything verbal, this can be both disputed and distorted.

xi. Do not use any products other than those for which you have received support. Should you run out of your sponsor's oil, make sure you borrow the same brand and don't forget 'big brother!'

Part C: The Pitfalls

Should parts A and B have appeared to you as little more than common sense, then I'm sure that this part will open many eyes. Most of the pitfalls I am about to describe have either concerned myself or have been recounted from the personal experience of others. All should be given serious consideration if your plans are to succeed and to become a continuing part of your life.

Assumptions

I'm sure we are all aware that the act of assumption in any dealing, business or otherwise, is one sure way of courting disaster. The danger in assuming anything relating to a sponsorship being that an indiscretion of this nature will inevitably lead to the participant's disillusionment and frustration. Do not under any circumstances take it for granted that you have finalised anything until the first cheque has been safely cleared.

Bargaining with your sponsor

Another major 'clanger!' It can be very tempting to use one prospect to hasten a sponsorship deal with another. However certain you are that such an action can do no harm, be assured that it will. Curb any temptation that might be there to play one prospective sponsor off against another; not only is it deception, but it can sometimes snowball leading to your reversing the situation. In one word, don't!

You can't chance losing both your prospects, along with your reputation.

Being bought

Finding out that you have been bought is one of the major problems allied to any financial arrangement which unites a business and a person or persons. Although it can work for a few 'top of the tree' subjects, by and large it is something to be avoided although difficult to detect until it has happened. What your sponsor has bought is a share of the action in which you act as an advertising/publicity medium. What they have not purchased is you, your club or your team. A sign that this phenomenon is about to happen is usually a tendency for the sponsor to stray from the terms agreed or to interfere with your side of the arrangements. Unless this is what you want, be careful; it can only lead to 'bad blood!'

Car traders

Mentioned briefly at the conclusion of Chapter four, car traders are seen by many as being a caravan, 'Arthur Daly' and a demolition site. Whilst it would be wrong to generalise I would nevertheless advise against any approach in this direction, since this end of the motor trade is not renowned for parting with money. In this respect I'm sure that most participants will agree that it usually winds up with the sponsor expecting more than they're prepared to give.

Exploitation

Anyone becoming involved in a promotions or publicity exercise has to accept that one of the hazards is the exploitation of their efforts and talents by those in the money seat. Worse still its symptoms can be hard to detect; therefore, be on your guard, accept that it does happen and all too regularly. Especially you should beware of the 'big' talker and enact the principal of being a good listener, it is just possible that you may realise that something is afoot and that it is something not in your interests.

Greed

I have seen at first hand the prospecti that have been submitted to numerous firms by all grades of motorsporting participant, varying from the novice to a few of almost international status. When budgeting they will seek everything from a sponsor without a thought of any self-contribution, whilst arguing that motorsport, although expensive, does attract a lot of publicity.

Value for money, the Peter Clements Shell Oils/Super Cleaners Talbot.

All that these competitors are doing is to damage the sport and themselves, in addition to making it very difficult for others. Be reasonable and remember that most of your colleagues do exercise tact and diplomacy in this direction. Greed is amongst the worst of all my sponsorship criticisms and can easily destroy an otherwise hopeful negotiation if, or when, discovered.

Grounds for divorce

Readers might think that this is a peculiar title for any 'pitfall' connected with motorsport. However, those of the male sex can derive comfort from the fact that it applies solely to the female participant in this particular context. One of the major drawbacks which can affect the serious sporting – or indeed even business – involvement of a wife has to be the 'unfortunate' fact that she has a husband. Many an aspiring sportswoman – including those with excellent track records – has at one time or another come up against the time established excuse 'why do you need a sponsor, can't hubby pay?' Thankfully there is a way of avoiding the drastic action of permanently terminating your marital relationship. Simply change your name as they do in the acting profession or revert to your maiden name; both are acceptable to the RAC's Motor Sports Association. There is however, one other 'pitfall' brought about by this action: watch out for the sponsor who takes a fancy to you ... the 'grounds' could become a reality.

The low key confidence trick

This one is more likely to be tried on by the bigger multi-nationals than by the smaller company. It amounts to the sponsor having led you to believe that there is a massive publicity programme surrounding your liaison and then one fine day you're waking up to find that you're not getting the hoped-for publicity, nor the expected response. As a result you'll spend hours racking your brains, or the committee's, in search of the answer to what has gone wrong? In short, nothing has gone wrong; your sponsor has decided, for one reason or another, to go 'low key.'

However, they won't tell you what they are up to and on the face of it all will appear to be well until the day you wake up. What you are likely to discover is that massive press coverage promised has in fact only been spread around one or two of the more junior nationals and a number of locals. The television coverage you envisaged will also have been localised along with the radio, whilst a number of expected personal appearances will not materialise and, seemingly, will not as much as warrant any kind of explanation. In a few words, something has cropped up to change your sponsor's plans, or the agreements made were merely words. Whatever it is, it is made perfectly clear that it is none of your business! If you get wind of this one, run; relinquish the sponsorship, repay any cash balance you still have and get out. You have either been conned out of your rights or the sponsor has broken their part of the contract.

The slow payer

One of the more frustrating aspects of any sponsorship liaison is the slow payer, although in this respect the trouble more often lies with the participant than with the sponsor. Make absolutely certain that the payment of your sponsorship has been tied up, water tight. Don't be afraid to hammer this home, it is what this subject is all about and only you can suffer if it is not to hand. It might be that the sponsor has overlooked this payment due to other pressures, in which case be quite frank and tell them that you need the cash; this is why your agreement or contract must include a clause specifically covering settlement dates which, in turn, must be binding. However, a word of warning: do not under any circumstances use one sponsor's money for an event that is being backed by another. This 'robbing of Peter to pay Paul' solution can very easily get out of control and in the long run it is much better to adopt the practice that no money means no entry!

The Press

Apart from those matters that I have already discussed, another hazard surrounds the local media. Try and cultivate a working relationship with its editors in both your own area as well as in that of your sponsor. This should enhance your prestige, in addition to the chances of a joint mention and can certainly do you no harm.

Sponsor not being named

Whatever the importance of the occasion, always try to get your sponsor a mention even if it is only as a part of an event commentary. Similarly, the same applies to the press; a local mention is better than none at all.

Sponsor sharing

Introducing a third party into any form of sponsorship is taboo! Quash any idea of a partnership on this basis with a capital 'Q', it simply cannot work and can open the door to the deliberate or inadvertent stealing of the sponsorship already donated by one or other of the participating parties. Take a tip from the hand of experience: this sort of liaison will destroy relationships quicker than anything. No matter how well thought of you are within the tripartite circle, it is a human failing to try and use the attributes and success of others for one's own betterment. You can be sure that any such arrangement will confirm that 'two's company and three's a crowd' with one of the parties ending up being the loser. Should a third party be vital to your venture, call in a complete outsider, but definitely not an 'insider!'

Sponsor stealing

I refer to item 'ix' at the end of Chapter seven. No doubt this will raise more than a few eyebrows, but it does happen and all too frequently. Sometimes the theft can be described as inadvertent, whilst sadly, it is sometimes deliberate. Whatever the reason, it is an essential factor not to be forgotten when drawing up a contract. Always include a clause that will forbid either yourself or your sponsor from entering into any discussion with another without the express knowledge and approval of each other, and during the currency of the contract.

The culprits come from all avenues of motorsport, although I must admit that in some cases the misdemeanours do genuinely occur inadvertently. However, having tried to temper this somewhat unethical situation we do have to face up to the fact that it does happen quite deliberately and all too often. Unfortunately no one can either physically, or specifically, point an accusing finger as to whether such behaviour is deliberate or not, but it is nevertheless the root cause of many a sponsor changing course in mid-season for one reason or another. The situation in which this sort of misappropriation occurs can be that singular occasion when your sponsor asks to show their products at one of your venues; for example:

Some years ago a sponsor of mine asked for permission to display a new and much publicised car at a Donington Park race meeting. I telephoned the organising club who, in turn, suggested that the vehicle might also be used as their official 'course car', if my sponsor would agree to a donation to the club funds of £300. Needless to say this suggestion was rejected. In consequence the new car was allocated a place in the paddock rarely visited by the public. The offending club official spent the entire meeting trying to get the 'course car' and the £300 from my sponsor's bewildered representative, even resorting to the offer of a good deal for next year if they would agree. Fortunately the company's managing director arrived and promptly informed the club's officer that a contract existed between us and that his firm were in no position to talk to them, not even about the following season. I have often wondered if this was why I didn't receive any regulations for their next race meeting!

Make certain that your contract protects you from this sort of thing. Many participants will claim that all is fair in motorsport and sponsorship; frankly this behaviour is downright dishonest. Of course fellow competitors will always try to muzzle in, so perhaps it is all a question of how to block anothers access to your sponsor ... somehow?

Taxi Advertising

This pitfall could perhaps be allied to the advertising agent. Most of you will be familiar with the infamous black cab and the fact that many display large adverts on their front doors. This is precisely what you are offering your prospective sponsor, although admittedly in conjunction with some sort of complex publicity package. In sponsorship terms the front doors of a car, together with its front wings offer the most lucrative exposure points advertising-wise; see if you can get a taxi sized decal on to your Formula Ford, whilst asking any 'Cabby' what he gets paid for his part in the arrangement? The answer is 'peanuts' by comparison to your requirements. Unfortu-nately this lot can be a real pain, especially if you are seeking your fortune in one of our bigger cities; you are likely to get a 'flea in your ear' if you are unlucky enough to approach any firm that has already been involved with 'Taxi Advertising.' Your argument that such a vehicle normally plies within a local area will also fall on deaf ears, so watch out for this menace.

Under-cutting

Once again a reminder. The candidate wants £3,500, the prospect offers half. Unless you are certain where to get the balance from; thank them for their offer, but no thank you!

Writing too little

Secretaries along with most students of the written word will argue that brevity breeds efficiency. Try telling W.D. & H.O. Wills that your name is 'John Smith,' that you drive in Formula Libre and that you need £60,000! In this respect disregard this rule and give your prospective sponsor something to get their teeth into, however brief.

My purpose in defining in detail the 'rules of the game' has been twofold; first, it is almost mandatory to observe certain elementary, but specific dos and don'ts if your quest for sponsorship is to succeed. Second, it is most essential that you are made aware of the other side of the coin and, in particular, about the unethical practices that sometimes infiltrate motorsport in all its guises.

Chapter 10

Sponsorship Through the Eyes of its Participants

How many times during a season do you hear the comment why can't I find a sponsor or the criticism that many British firms seem reluctant to sponsor anyone or anything? In a lot of these cases the participant either hasn't tried or doesn't possess the required track record, since it can be both argued and substantiated that many British firms do support sport in its many costumes. Why then are such remarks passed and how does the average British company view the subject of sponsorship?

Nine times out of ten those that say they can't find a sponsor can be categorised as being one of the following:

i. The also ran: has little or no chance of being an attractive sponsorship proposition. In fairness, the fault might lie with the participant's choice of car or choice of event every bit as much as with his, or her, efforts. In such a case you should indulge in a little self-analysis and then set about putting the fault right, wherever it lies.

ii. Dad's got the money, but I want to do it myself: Entirely the wrong attitude. Proving yourself sponsor-worthy will come a lot easier with his help, I assure you.

iii. Everyone's doing better than me: If only I had a sponsor I could perform on equal terms. So and so's got a much better prepared car due to sponsorship; if

only. My advice to you is to go out and look for a sponsor and to face up to the fact that they won't come looking for you.

iv. How will a sponsor know if I'm any good: They won't know unless you've prepared a proper outline of your efforts to date and unless you're able to go on proving that your track record is no fluke.

v. I can't find the time: If you want sponsoring badly enough then you'll make the time. It all depends on your sincerity.

vi. I can't stand writing letters: You're not alone here. My advice is to get yourself a sponsorship or publicity agent, but please don't forget to pay them.

vii. I haven't got the confidence to talk to Paul Getty: In your case, prepare the necessary background work and then find an agent to act for you. Alternatively, why not ask Dad; he could save you a fee.

viii. I'm not sure if I'm ready: If you really don't know, then I hope I'm not around when you mistake Becketts for Abbey!

ix. Despite trying, I just can't sell myself: In your case you have one of two problems. First, you might not be approaching the challenge properly or second, it could be that you are over-selling yourself by simply talking too much.

Having described the negative attitudes of some of motorsports competitors, just how is sponsorship viewed by the more celebrated and successful participant? To make such an answer simple I need only refer to the author of this book's 'Foreword' – World Endurance Champion, Derek Bell. He says, I quote: "Raising sponsorship will always be difficult but having found a sponsor do look after him, so many people don't, much to the detriment of our sport." Unquote. In a nutshell, one of the Masters of our sport admits it is anything but easy for anyone to find a

sponsor, whilst indicating that keeping one is even harder.

Provided that you can answer most of the questions asked in Chapter three positively, you should find that the world of sponsorship is your oyster. However, standing around the circuits or stages bemoaning your lot will not bring you a sponsor, anymore than it will turn you into another Derek Bell.

Now for the prospective sponsors: how do they look upon the participant? In short they will more often than not treat you in one of three ways as follows:

1. With contempt
You may have to face up to this one sometime. There are still many top management executives who do not believe in

The 'Dick Barbour Racing' Porsche must be viewed favourably by its sponsors, clarity being paramount. Photographed during the Le Mans 24 Hour Race.

any sort of progress that can be directly attributed to our American cousins, although no doubt even these dyed in the wool types will be replaced one day with the influx of new and younger blood. In the meantime however, hold on to your hat; you'll either get a sharp rebuff, a letter accusing you of begging or more often still, nothing! This is the prospect most likely to deposit your handiwork in the waste bin, despite your request for its return pre-paid.

2. With curiosity

Rather like the window shopper, this style of sponsor will give you the 'run around' and will waste your time. All they want is an insight into sponsorship and its place in sport generally. They may have honest intentions for the future, but for the present they will waste your time or finish up offering you a pittance in the hope of plenty from you. In the event of your coming across a company in this category, there are four surefire indications that you are being 'taken', as follows:

First indication, you will suddenly realise that you have never come face to face with 'Mr. Big.' He's always either away, in a meeting or otherwise engaged. You will be continuously fobbed off with the statement that he is aware of all that is going on, but that your contact has been authorised to deal with the negotiation; don't you believe it, your contact has no such authority whatsoever. This one will offer you the same £75 that was once offered to me.

Second indication, your contact, or whoever, will make the observation that your programme is too national or too local. Since the basis of your competing was made known in your prospectus, which has been in your would-be sponsor's hands for some time, you must in this case assume that this firm are solely out for information. Ask for the return of your correspondence with the comment that you are sorry that they have wasted *your* time.

Third indication, the company continually ask what each part of your car is worth in advertising terms, despite the fact that this is clearly defined and shown in your budget breakdown. This sponsor is looking for a cheap get out; so you get out!

Fourth indication, you may be asked to provide passes to an event so that the company can come along and assess your potential. They might even suggest, subtly, that you display a small decal. On the day in question the firm's Managing Director will turn up at the 'Knowsley Stages' with his family and at least another half dozen or so hangers on. You will be introduced as 'our driver, the one I told you we are going to sponsor.' Frankly they are not thinking of doing anything of the sort; in fact they have just had all the use out of you that they ever wanted. If you fall for this ruse make your objections known, but for the moment go along with the 'ploy.' After the event take the offending MD to one side and inform him that you don't like his methods and that his reference to your being 'their driver' has just cost him £x for which his company will be duly invoiced. This type of prospect is trying to show off at your expense.

All the examples used are based on fact, in short, all that a 'curious' sponsor is looking for is a mug! Fortunately they can be recognised as indicated and probably think they are missing out on sponsorship until they count the cost.

3. With genuine interest

Instantly recognisable, this firm makes all the right noises and will immediately instil you with confidence. They will reply to your approach letter promptly; simply asking you to contact Mr. So and So's secretary for an appointment, with nothing, at this stage, either implied or suggested. Nevertheless, there will be that indefinable 'something' that tells you that all could be well if you play your cards right. Similarly, the ensuing meeting will be conducted with enthusiasm, they will tell you about their company, they will tell you

John Foulston's McLaren M19 still wears the logo of its one-time successful liaison with 'Yardley for Men'.

about their marketing policy and will then ask you to talk about yourself and your plans. Having listened, they will next enter into a detailed discussion of your prospectus and the effectiveness of any union that may result.

The executives with whom you will be dealing will all know their subject and when reaching a decision about you, this will be both definite and final. Lastly, they will be eager to learn about your part, should they react in your favour, and will expect you to live up to it. However, if this prospect does turn you down you will be left in no doubt that their interest in you was genuine; something that is inexplicable, but that you will instinctively know was there.

Before my summing up, I would like to stress, once again, that any successful sponsorship negotiation is dependent upon honesty and trust on the part of both parties. Unfortunately, in keeping with any monetary transaction there are those whose actions are anything but scrupulous. From the participant's standpoint it is the means with which to find out who the latter are, that is vital to your success. On the other hand your sponsor will want to know how much further your intentions go beyond that of your simply needing the money.

Good luck!

Author's Summary

Anyone who has applied to the RAC's Motor Sporting Association for one or another of its competition licences, will know that the fee includes a copy of the famous 'Blue Book'. To give this publication its full title, it is the RAC/MSA's British Motor Sports Yearbook and within its 300 odd pages can be found the many complex rules and regulations which govern every aspect of our sport. That it is complex cannot be denied, but nevertheless no one can contemplate competing at any level without having first perused its relevant sections; the word 'relevant' being the operative one. Similar applies to any quest for sponsorship in that it is all a matter of separating the wheat from the chaff.

When a participant sets out on a sponsor hunt he, or she, is about to enter the complex world of marketing. A world made more difficult owing to the item you are selling being of the intangible variety. Consequently therefore, anyone embarking upon this venture must, like the perusal of the RAC Yearbook, separate the negatives from the positives.

I was once told by an encyclopaedia salesman that ninety percent of his problems, when confronting a prospective customer, revolved around his disposal of the many and varied objections which were put to him. This somewhat fundamental requirement of any marketing exercise is now a part of most business school courses, and must likewise be employed when contemplating your search for the illusive sponsor.

For example, there is no use attempting to get support for the 'Unipart Saloon Car Championship' if you have no saloon car track record. There is no use your trying to get support for your club, if your ideas are no more imaginative than those of the other clubs in your area who have already skimmed the cream from the milk. Finally, there is no use your trying to sell your sponsorship ideas for a national rally based in a Welsh town if the same town already supports its own car club, an Eisteddfod, soccer team and rugby club. Like the esteemed encyclopaedia salesman, much hard work can be taken out of your hunt if you first get rid of the many things that can thwart your efforts. In other words make sure, before you go through any doors or put pen to paper, that you have virtually placed the prospective sponsor in the position of being unable to say no!

By taking those parts of this book which apply to your own particular sponsorship problem and acting upon the advice given therein conscientiously, you should be able to reduce the chances of a negative reply almost one hundredfold. Similarly, I have seen fit to draw your attention to the many things that can go wrong, including dishonesty among both your fellows and companies that should know better. This again is intended to help you towards a much better understanding of the subject.

Sponsorship is a relatively new angle of

the publicity game, which some see as yet another Americanism violating the European way of life. Make allowances if some firms seem reluctant to indulge; fortunately it is a growing medium and although demanding patience and tena-city, it can reveal many companies who are quite willing to become involved for the returns offered.

Remember, 'if at first you don't succeed ... keep trying!'

APPENDIX N

Some Successful Sponsorships, past and present

Andrews Heat for Hire	International Rallying	Vauxhall.
Autolec Ltd	Autotests	Championship sponsor.
Avon Tyres Ltd	Formula 3000	The Onyx Team.
Canon Photographic	World Endurance Racing	Porsche.
Castrol Sport	Rallycross	The Peacock Team.
Daily Express	International Karting	Co-organiser British GP.
Dickens Tools	Autotests	Event sponsor.
Esso Petroleum	National Rallying	Scottish Rally series.
Hermetite	International Karting	British Kart GP.
John Players Special	Formula One	Team Lotus.
Leicestercard	Speed Hillclimbing	Bill Wood, Mallock U2.
Marlboro' Cigarettes	Formula One	McLaren International.
Martini & Rossi	World Endurance Racing	Lancia/Abarth.
Motorcraft	Celebrity Racing	Ford.
Otford Group	Thundersport Series	Mike Wilds, Lola.
Pace Petroleum	Sprinting	BARC LHCC Championship sponsor.
Pipercross Competition	International Rallying	Trade support, Russell Brookes.
The Quick Group	Sprint Championship	Lancashire & Cheshire Car Club.
Rothmans Tobacco	International Rallying	The Opel Team.
Shell UK Oils	National Rallying	Autosport series sponsor.
Uniroyal	Saloon Car Racing	Championship sponsor.
Waring & Gillow Maples	Speed Hillclimbing	Alastair Douglas-Osborne.
Warmastyle	Formula Three	Russell Spence, Ralt.
Wendy Wools	Saloon Car Racing	BARC championship sponsor.
Yardley for Men	Formula One	BRM and McLaren International Racing.